RÛMÎ AND SUFISM

Rûmî and Sufism

by

Eva de Vitray-Meyerovitch

Translated from the French
by
Simone Fattal

The Post-Apollo Press
Sausalito, California

© Les Editions du Seuil. 1977.
© Simone Fattal for the English edition 1987.

Published by the Post-Apollo Press, 35 Marie Street, Sausalito, California 94965.

Originally published in French under the title:
Rûmî et le Soufisme.

Cover design by Simone Fattal
Composed by Michael Sykes at Archetype West,
Point Reyes, California
Manufactured in the United States.

Library of Congress Cataloging-in-Publication Data

Vitray-Meyerovitch, Eva de.
  Rûmî and Sufism.

  Translation of: Rumi et le soufisme.
  Bibliography: p. 166.167.
  Includes index.
  1. Mevleviyeh. 2. Jalâl-al-Dîn Rûmî, Maulana,
1207–1273 — Religion. 3. Sufism. I. Title.
BP189.7.M4V5713 1987 297'.4'0924 87-62177
ISBN 0-942996-08-9

Reprinted 1989
Printed on Acid Free Paper

RÛMÎ AND SUFISM

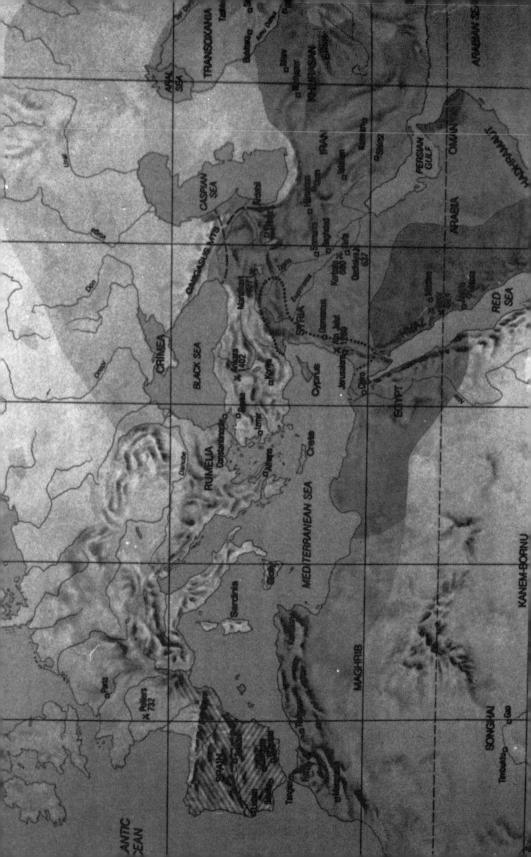

Table of Contents

Illustrations

A.A.A. Photos : 154. — Archives of the Author : 162. — Bibliothèque Nationale :
19, 86, 90, 103, 130. — Bodleian Library : 122. — Arnaud Desjardins : 155.
— Léonard Freed/Magnum : 14/15, 25, 72/73, cover photo and 114/115,
146/147. — Roland Michaud : 20, 21, 22, 29, 34, 39, 40, 45, 48, 54, 59, 66, 68, 76,
82, 93, 100, 105, 108, 134, 139, 143, 152, 164/165. — Giraudon : 127.
Michael Gilsenan, *Saint and Sufi in modern Egypt* (1973) : 158.

The tables on pages 95 and 111 have been established by Pierre-Louis Hardy.

The maps on pages 8 and 60 have been graciously lent by the Mill Valley Public
Library of Mill Valley, California.

INTRODUCTION

A man of his time and of all times, that was Djalâl-od-Dîn Rûmî, a living and brotherly presence throughout the Islamic world with its 800 million inhabitants. From Cairo to Tangiers, from Djakarta to Lahore, in the humblest villages of India, Afghanistan, Iran and Turkey, his poems are chanted by the crowds during the pilgrimages. As far away as Bosnia-Herzegovina his memory is still revered. In Istanbul there is a cemetery near which the "lovers of Rûmî" want to be buried. There were at least a hundred thousand disciples before World War II, with monasteries throughout the Orient and into the Balkans, and chairs where, for seven centuries, his doctrine has been taught. It is acknowledged by the Orientalists that he is the greatest mystical poet of all times and by the Easterners that he is second only to the Koran. He was a seer who wrote, at the time of Saint Louis, that if one cut an atom one would find in it a solar system in miniature and who knew, three centuries before Copernicus, not only that the earth turned around the sun, but that there were nine planets, a discovery not made in the West until 1930.

But most of all, Djalâl-od-Dîn gave a message of a burning actuality founded on personal experience. This message came from a man who, though he became a saint, was not a cleric. He had borne all the vicissitudes of a tormented epoch ravaged by wars and calamities. He was exiled from his country, was widowed very young with infants, lost, under the blows of murderers (among whom was his own son), the spiritual master he loved more than himself, and yet Rûmî testified that life has a meaning, that love and joy transcend all sorrow and that, in the end, nothing is absurd because "man is infinitely greater than man."

Having reached the metaphysical realization which leaves no doubt, Rûmî wanted to be a master of *awakening.* He transmitted a teaching founded on *knowledge,* using methods which have proven their worth. He embodied his teaching in the most beautiful form, beauty being also mediatory.

The content of his teaching is Sufism, which constitutes, not a doctrine, but a Way. It is taught inside a *tarîqa* (order or brotherhood) such as the one he created in the 13th century in Anatolia and which spread throughout the immense Ottoman Empire. That order, similar to the Christian Third Orders, gave the Islamic world several scientists, artists and poets, and, until Atatürk, it was the master of this order who gave the sultân his investiture.

Dervishes in Konya ▶

The Master,
his life, his order,
his works

Djalâl-od-Dîn Rûmî: his life, his epoch

According to all his biographers, Muhammad Djalâl-od-Dîn was commonly called Khodâvendegâr (that is how his son addressed him), or Mawlânâ Khodâvendegâr, which means "Our Master." His father, struck by his precocious sainthood, gave him that name when he was still a child. He is called thus throughout Turkey (pronounced in the Turkish way, Mawlâna). It is usually followed by "from Rum" (Anatolia) because that is where he spent most of his life. He is known all over the Islamic world under the name Rûmî.

The epoch in which he was born was one of the most troubled times in history. "This century is one of grandiose duels: struggles between the clergy and the Empire, struggles between the East and the West, struggle which seems eternal between Iran and Touran. In 1190, Frederic Barbarossa died in the Crusade, soon after the whole of Europe took sides with either the Pope or the Emperor. . . In the East, the Christian domination was displaced; by the end of the 13th century, Salah-od-Dîn had, little by little, pushed the Franks toward the coast. After the loss of Edessa, they retained only the kingdom of Jerusalem, the county of Tripoli and the principality of Antioch. . . At the same time Persia (the native country of Djalâl-od-Dîn) was bearing, once more, the disgrace of invasion. This time the conquerors did not come from Arabia as in the 8th century, but instead from the distant Orient. The Empire of Khwarazm (his native country) fell in its turn. Iran plunged into the tornado that, after having submerged Oriental Asia, destroyed the Baghdad Califate and swept over Central Europe. It was an epoch of chaos and uncertainty." (Henri Massé, *Essay on the poet Saadi*).

It is very difficult to differentiate between history and legend in the biography of Mawlânâ Djalâl-od-Dîn. The information we are giving therefore comes from contemporary sources, or those which immediately follow the master's death. He was born, probably, on September 30th, 1207 in Balkh, a town in Khorassan celebrated for its beauty. In that province, which was the cradle of Persian civilization where men like Ferdowsi, Avicenna and Al-Ghazâlî were born, Djalâl-od-Dîn's family was one of the most prominent. His father, a Sufi master and theologian, was also an eloquent preacher who had numerous disciples. Known under the name Bahâ-od-Dîn Walad and nicknamed "The Sultân of Scientists," he had been born in 1148 and died in 1231 in Konya.

Fearing the Mongol invasion, he left Balkh quickly with his family in 1219. One year later Rûmî's hometown was totally destroyed. Bahâ-od-Dîn first took his family to Mecca to perform the pilgrimage. In Nishâpûr they met the great mystic poet, Farîd-od-Dîn 'Attâr, and the latter offered the young Djalâl-od-Dîn his *Book of Secrets* and predicted, according to the sources, that soon he would light a fire in the hearts of all mystic lovers. All his life Djalâl-od-Dîn retained a great admiration for 'Attar. He used to say, "He has crossed the seven cities of Love, whereas I am still at the corner of a narrow street."

On their way back from Mecca they settled in Arzanjân, a small Armenian town which belonged to the dynasty of Al-e-Menkujak. In 625 (hegira) Arzanjân was conquered by 'Alâ-od-Dîn Kaykobâd Seldjukide, the man who was to invite Djalâl-od-Dîn's family to Konya later. But, before that, they spent some time in Laranda, the present town of Karaman. Aflâkî, the hagiographer of the brotherhood, relates those events in this way:

"After going from post-house to post-house, Bahâ-od-Dîn arrived in Laranda, which was a dependence of Konya. At that time a good servant of Islam, 'Ala'-od-Dîn Kaykobâd, also called Emir Moussa, lived there and was the prefect of the town and its governor. He was a Turk and his heart was simple, brave and sincere. When he learned that such a personality was arriving from the Khorassan, he walked toward him, followed by all the citizens and soldiers, to welcome him. When they arrived in his presence, they all became his disciples. In spite of an invitation to settle in the palace, the saint did not accept the governor's offer but asked to be taken to a college. Emir Moussa ordered that a college be built in the middle of the town, a college where it is said that the saint lived for seven years. When Djalâl-od-Dîn became a young man he was married to the daughter of Hodja Cherif-od-Dîn Lala of Samarkand. The latter was a respected man of noble origin. He had a daugh-

The taking of Baghdad by the Mongols in 1258 (14th c. miniature).

Balkh: The mosque of the nine domes (10th c.).

ter who was extremely beautiful and gracious, unequaled in education
and perfection, named Gauher-Khâtoun.

"A magnificent wedding took place in 623 (1226). Sultân Walad and
'Alâ-od-Dîn Tchelebi were born of that union."

The narrator goes on to say that after a long stay in this town, the
Sultân invited Bahâ-od-Dîn Walad to Konya. "He came to meet him
with a big escort, stepped down from his horse and kissed the sheikh's
knee. As long as the Sultân lived he bestowed upon him honors and
respect. During his last illness the Sultân went to visit him and wept a
lot. Bahâ-od-Dîn told him not to cry for he would soon join him. The
Sultân did actually die a few years later."

Bahâ-od-Dîn Walad took up his role as a preacher and teacher again
in Konya. When he died Djalâl-od-Dîn, only 24 years old, replaced
him. A year later an old disciple of his father, Burhân-od-Dîn
Muhaqqîq Tirmidhi, came to see his old master. Having found that he
was dead, he stayed near Djalâl-od-Dîn and became his spiritual master
for nine years. He sent the young man to Aleppo to study because it was
a flourishing cultural center. Then Djalâl-od-Dîn went to Damascus
where he stayed for many years. One of the greatest mystics and thinkers, Muhyî-od-Dîn Ibn-ul-'Arabî, was spending the last years of his life
there. Rûmî had already met him when he had arrived in Damascus as a

The Khorassan.

child with his father. It is said that when Ibn-ul-'Arabî saw the young Djalâl-od-Dîn walking behind Bahâ-od-Dîn, he exclaimed: "Glory be to God, an ocean is walking behind a lake."

After an absence of seven years, Rûmî came back to Konya and settled at his college. From 1240 to 1244 he taught Law and religious canon there and gave spiritual guidance. His career as a teacher seemed assured until an event occurred that disrupted his life and made him a mystic burned with Divine Love. He, himself, described thus what happened to him: "I was raw, then I got cooked and now I am burned." It is, indeed, a language of fire that he used from then on. He would say: "It is a burn of the heart that I want, it is this burn which is everything, more precious than a worldly empire, because it calls God, secretly, in the night." (*Mathnawî,* III, 203)

The event that changed his life was the meeting of a strange wandering dervish, Shams of Tabrîz. Then about 60 years of age, Shams had spent his life in constant peregrinations, praying to God to let him meet one of his saints and offering in exchange, his own life. He then received the revelation to go to Asia Minor.

He arrived in Konya on the 29th of November, 1244. He stayed at the caravanserail of the sugar merchants where he locked himself up in a miserable room and engaged completely in mortifications. The circumstances surrounding his first encounter with Djalâl-od-Dîn have been described differently by the various historians. According to one of them, Rûmî was going out of his college situated in the cotton trader's market and was on his way to the bazaar, riding his mule. His students were following him on foot. Suddenly, Shams ran up to him, held the mule's bridle and asked him: "Who was the greatest, Bâyazîd or Muhammad?" Mawlânâ answered that it was a strange question, Muhammad being the seal of the prophets. "What is the meaning then," answered Shams, "of this: the Prophet said to God: 'I have not known Thee as I should have,' and of Bâyazîd saying: 'Glory be to me! How high is my dignity!'" Mawlânâ fainted. When he recovered his senses he took Shams by the hand and led him to the college on foot where they kept to themselves, in a cell, for 40 days.

However, Muhyî-od-Dîn 'Abd-al-Qâdir (696-775 hegira), the contemporary of Sultân Walad, Rûmî's son, tells the story differently in his book *Al-Kawâkib-ul-Mudî'ah*. "One day Mawlânâ was sitting at home surrounded with his students and his books. Shams-od-Dîn entered, saluted him and asked, pointing to the books: "What are these?" Mawlânâ answered: "You do not know it." He had hardly pronounced these words when fire fell on the books and they burned. Mawlânâ asked: "What is that?" Shams answered: "You don't know it," and left. Mawlânâ then left his family and went to look for Shams.

Another version of that meeting, according to Djâmî, says that when Shams arrived in Konya, Rûmî was sitting by a fountain and he had deposited his books near him. Shams asked: "What are these?" Mawlânâ answered: "These are words. Why should you care about them?" Shams threw all the books into the water. Mawlânâ exclaimed: "What did you do? In some of these books were important manuscripts by my father that cannot be found anywhere else." Shams plunged his hand into the water and took the books out one by one and none of them were wet. Mawlânâ asked: "What is this secret?" Shams answered: "That is called *dhawq* (desire for God) and *hâl* (spiritual state). Why should you care about these things?" And they left together.

For still others, the question that Shams asked was this one: "What is the purpose of the spiritual efforts and mortifications, of repeating the prayers and of knowledge?" Mawlânâ answered: "To understand the tradition and the religious customs." Shams said: "All this is external." Mawlânâ then said: "What is there beyond that?" Shams answered: "Knowledge is to cross from the unknown into the known." And then he recited these verses form Sanâ'i's *Diwân:*

> "If knowledge does not liberate the self from the self
> then ignorance is better than such knowledge."

Mawlânâ fell at Shams's feet and renounced his teaching.

It is difficult to know exactly what happened, perhaps the best thing may be to refer to the *Walad-Nâma* by Sultân Walad who declares simply that his father was looking for a spiritual master, a *pir,* but does not say how he met him.

In fact, the whole work and the whole life of Rûmî became the echo of the bedazzlement of that meeting.

"The seeker," writes Sultân Walad, speaking about this quest for the Divine Beloved by his father, "is the one who finds. . . For the Beloved becomes the lover. His supreme guide on the mystical path had been Shams of Tabrîz. God consented that Shams should manifest himself to him particularly and that it should be for him alone. . . Nobody would have been worthy of such a vision. After such a long wait Mawlânâ saw Shams's face and the secrets became as clear to him as the daylight. He saw Him, whom cannot be seen, he heard what nobody had ever heard from anyone before. . .He fell in love with Him and was annihilated." (*Walad-Nâma,* p. 41)

Comparing the Absolute to an ocean without borders, a Reality in which every individual existence is but an ephemeral manifestation, Rûmî describes in one of his most beautiful poems, (*Mystic Odes* 649) the rapture of the soul which discovers its own identity with the Divine. "Every drop of the sea is embodied in an apparent form." He says somewhere else: "Knowst with certitude that his name is Djonayd or Bayâzîd." (*Mystic Odes,* 583). In choosing these two names, those of two of the greatest mystics of Islam, Rûmî wanted to show that the souls which had become capable of being a Divine Image and the Mirror of the Supreme Reality, can become guides for the mystical pilgrims.

> "Without the salvation-bearing help of my Lord Shams-ul-Haqq of Tabriz
> None can contemplate the moon or become the sea."
>
> (*Mystic Odes,* 649)

Konya: Seldjoukide monument.

Because Shams appeared one day in the life of Rûmî as one of those Divine envoys who, as he put it, "takes the soul by the neck" to tear it from its lethargic state and pushes it toward seeking God, he maintained a boundless love and gratitude for him all his life.

When the spiritual master has thus awakened the heart, asleep until then,

"An image crosses the heart: 'Return to your origin.'
The heart flutters all around and away from the world of colours and perfumes,
Clamoring: 'Wherefore the Origin?'
while tearing apart its adornments, because of its love."

(*Mystic Odes*, 18)

The name Shams means "sun" and Rûmî enjoys playing on this theme.

"The sun of Shams-od-Dîn, the glory of Tabrîz,
has not shone on anything perishable without making it eternal."

(*Mystic Odes*, 861)

Being at the same time the mediator and the personifier of Love, Shams was to make Rûmî discover that all duality can be transcended because every being "possesses another dimension." (*Mystic Odes*, 1038). Therefore it was this Shams-od-Dîn, "eternal and supreme," who, as he knew it, resided in the innermost of his being.

"The Beloved said: 'I am your own soul and your own heart,
Why are you so stricken with terror?"

(*Mystic Odes*, 1022)

Had he not also said:

"I came to take you by the hand
To deprive you of your heart and your self and settle you
In the Heart and in the Soul.
I came in the midst of a beautiful spring, O rosebush!
To surround you with my arms and hold you.
I came to invest you, in this abode, with splendor,
I am carrying you to the heights of the heavens,
Like the prayer of all the Beloved."

(*Mystic Odes*, 322)

After they had spent sixteen months together, Shams decided to go to Damascus for he was constantly attacked by Rûmî's disciples who were jealous of his influence on their master's mind. Djalâl-od-Dîn, deeply afflicted, sent his son, Sultân Walad, to beg him to come back to Konya. Shams accepted but the persecutions started again and on the third of December, 1247, Shams disappeared; murdered, it was said. It is even confirmed that one of Rûmî's sons, 'Ala-od-Dîn, was among the murderers. Mawlânâ, nevertheless, did not seem to know that his friend had died. The fact must have been well concealed. He went twice to Damascus in the hope of finding him again. He was not be be consoled for a long time and wrote on Shams's cell door:

> I was snow, under your rays I did melt;
> Earth drank me; fog of spirit,
> I climb back the road to the Sun.

It is after this disappearance that Rûmî instituted the spiritual concert known as the *samâ,* which represented for him, not only a religious ceremony, but also the spontaneous manifestation of emotions. Sultân Walad describes him thus:

> He never stopped listening to music and dancing;
> He rested neither in the day nor at night.
> He had been a scholar, he became a poet.
> He had been an ascetic, he became drunk with love,
> Not from the wine of the grape: the illuminated soul
> Drinks nothing but the wine from the Light.

He composed, in the memory of his beloved master, the collection of Odes which bears his name: *Diwân Shams-e-Tabrîzi,* which is composed of admirable songs of "love and sorrow." It is an immense work consecrated to this love, terrestrial in appearance, but which, in reality, is an hypostasis of the Divine Love. We find all through these poems, the ever-present pain and the echo of the grief caused by the first separation:

> O Master, come! O Master, come! O Lord, return!
> Do not keep me longing, do not keep me longing!
> O Master, clever and beautiful, come! . . .
> O night disturbed, disappear! O unspeakable sorrow, Away from me!
> O subdued intelligence, let yourself be vanished!
> O lucid fullness, come!
> O uncertain heart, come! O wounded soul, come!
>
> (*Mystic Odes,* 36)

> O Love who devours the heart, O Master, protect me!
> You are like Noah, my savior, you are my soul, you are the winner
> and the vanquished,
> You are the wounded heart, and I am in front of the door of Secrets.
> You are the light, you are the joy, you are fortune triumphant!
> You are the bird of Mount Sinai and I have been wounded by your beak.
> You are the drop of water and you are the ocean, you are the grace
> and you are the fury,
> You are the sugar and you are the poison, do not torture me furthermore!
>
> (*Mystic Odes,* 37)

His son and confidant tells us that Rûmî was nevertheless able to transcend his sorrow by internalizing this specific love which represented, in his eyes, the face of Divine Love.

"Although Mawlânâ has apparently not found Shams of Tabrîz, he has found him in himself because they shared the same spiritual state (*hâl*). He said:

"Although we are far from him in the flesh — without body or soul, we are both one and the same light — you can see him, if you so desire, or you can see me. I am him, he is me, O seeker! Why do I say me or him, when he is myself and I am he? Yes, all is him and I am contained in him. . . As I am he, what am I looking for? I am him now and I am speaking of myself. Certainly it is myself I was seeking." (*Walad-Nâma*, p. 60)

A poem from the Diwân translates this feeling:

Happy is the time when we sit in the palace, you and I,
With two forms and two faces, but a single soul, you and I.
The colours of the grove and the voices of the birds will bestow immortality
The moment we will enter the garden, you and I!
The stars of the heavens will come to look at us:
We will show them the moon itself, you and I.
You and I, liberated from ourselves, will be united in ecstasy,
Joyful and with no idle words, you and I.
The birds of the heavens will have their hearts eaten by envy
In that place where we will laugh happily, you and I!
But the great marvel is that, you and I, huddled in the same nest,
Are in fact and in this instant, the one in Iraq, the other in
Khorassan, you and I.

(*Mystic Odes*)

Therefore, all duality being transcended, the interior master and the exterior one are one and the same. *"Anâ aqûlu wa-anâ asma'u wa-laysa fi'l dâri ghayri dayyârun."* "I am the one speaking and I am the one listening, and there is no one in the house but me."

"In your own self, the seer and the seen are one and the same."

(*Mystic Odes*, V)

Something else remains to be said, but it will be told by the
Holy Spirit, without me.
Or rather, you will be the one to say it to your own ear —
neither me, nor someone other than me, will say it to you,
O you who are my own self!

(*Mathnawî*, III, 1298 s.)

In the sky, a moon appeared, at dawn,
She descended from the sky and threw her glance to me,
Like a falcon taking hold of a bird, during the hunt,
She seized me and took me high in the skies.
When I looked at me I did not see me
Because in this moon, my body, by grace, had become the soul.
When I traveled within the soul, I only saw the moon,

The meeting of Shams and Rûmî (16th c. miniature).

Until was unveiled to me the mystery of eternal Theophany.
The nine celestial spheres were totally immersed in this moon.
The hull of my being was totally hidden in that sea.
The sea broke down in waves; Intelligence returned
And made its call: that's how it was and had been.
The sea got covered with foam, and from each fluff of foam
Something appeared as a form, something appeared as a body.
Each fluff of foam which looked like a body received a signal from that sea,
Melted immediately and followed the course of the waves.
Without the salvation-bearing help of my Lord Shams-ul-Haqq of Tabrîz,
None can contemplate the moon, nor become the sea.

(*Mystic Odes*, 649)

At the end, you left, you went to the Invisible.
O marvel! O marvel! By which way did you go out of this world?
You frantically shook your wings and your feathers and, breaking your cage,
You took off and left for the world of the Soul.
You were a noble falcon in an old woman's barn:
When you heard the call of the drum you went beyond space.
You were the possessed nightingale among the owls:
The scent of the rose garden reached you and you went to the garden.
You felt weary of this bitter world:
At the end, you left for Eternity's Tavern.
You went like an arrow to the target of felicity,
For that aim, like an arrow, you left the arc.
The world had sent you wrong messages,
You left the signs and went toward that which has no signs.
When you have become the Sun why would you need a crown?
Why ask for a belt, when you left the here and now?
I heard that you became all eyes, and that you look toward the soul;
Why look toward the soul, when you left for the Soul of the soul?
O Heart, what a strange bird you are, looking after praise!
Using your twin wings as a shield, you left for the lance.
Flowers flee Autumn, but you, which strange flower are you
Who, wilting, wilting, have left for the autumn wind!
Fallen from the sky, like rain on the roof of this terrestrial world
You ran in all directions and left through the eaves.
Keep quiet, forsake the trouble of talking; do not fall asleep,
You who took refuge near such a tender Beloved.

(*Mystic Odes*)

AFTER THE DISAPPEARANCE OF SHAMS

After he had lost all hope of finding Shams in this world, Rûmî chose
as a friend and master of his disciples, Salâh-od-Dîn Farîdûn Zarkûb,
who had also been a disciple of Burhân-od-Dîn Muhaqqiq Tirmidhî.
He lived in the outskirts of Konya and one day came into town as Mawlânâ was preaching in the mosque and quoting their common master.

Salâh-od-Dîn got up and fell at Rûmî's feet. They became inseparable until Salâh-od-Dîn's death in 657 (hegira) which came ten years later. Sultân Walad, Rûmî's son, married Fâtima Khâtûn, Salâh-od-Dîn's daughter. Sultân Walad tells us: "Thanks to him, the upheaval in Mawlânâ's life receded and his pains and complaints were somewhat appeased. Mawlânâ was with him like he was with the other king, Shams of Tabrîz. His eyes were constantly fixed on him. Except for him, everything was void for Mawlânâ."

Again the disciples became jealous. They did not respect Salâh-od-Dîn, who was but a simple artisan whose trade was gilding and illuminating (*Zarkûb*). They said to each other: "We were saved from the other one. All being said we fell into a trap. This one is worse than the first one . . . He does not possess the art of writing nor has he science or eloquence. He is an ignorant."

But Salâh-od-Dîn possessed the real science which is the science of the things of God, wrote Sultân Walad. Upon learning that the disciples were planning to kill him, he smiled: "I am but a mirror in front of Mawlânâ. It is in me that he sees his own face. If he chose me it is because he chose himself." Mawlânâ refers to the hostility of his disciples, notably in *The Book of Inner Knowledge* (ch. 22, in Arabic), and cites often Salâh-od-Dîn's name in the *Diwân* dedicated to Shams of Tabrîz. Salâh-od-Dîn's funeral was accompanied by a *samâ'* and he is buried next to Rûmî's father.

Mawlânâ chose Husâm-od-Dîn Tchelebî as the next master of his disciples. He held him in the greatest esteem and claims that it is thanks to his demands that he composed his celebrated *Mathnawi*. One day after they had read works by 'Attar and Sanâ'î together, Husâm-od-Dîn suggested that he should also compose a treatise in verse containing his teachings. Rûmî replied that he had already thought about it and took a piece of paper from his turban on which were written the first 18 distichs. Thus began the writing of the *Mathnawî;* Mawlânâ improvising and Husâm-od-Dîn writing down the verses and reciting them. The writing sometimes went on all night. It was interrupted after the completion of the first volume by the death of Husâm-od Dîn's wife and taken up again two years later in 662 (hegira). It probably went on until Rûmî's death in 672.

THE GOLDEN LEGEND

A climate of legend surrounds Rûmî's life. Most of what we know comes from Aflâkî, the hagiographer of the brotherhood. The anecdotes he relates are often best approached with caution. Yet, in spite of the exaggerations which abound in this kind of relation, we find traits which we feel are accurate and which create a portrait as loving as *Fioretti's*. There were many common traits between Rûmî and St. Francis of Assisi who died when the master of Konya was 19. They had the same love for the humble and the poor and the same urge for putting a sacred cosmos in unison. "The trees," Rûmî used to say, "recognize me and answer my salutations."

One day his friends had formed a circle on the banks of a pond. "Our master," relates Aflâkî, "engulfed in an ocean of light, was telling us the thoughts of the Outer World. By chance all the frogs in the pond started to croak together. Our master shouted to them in a frightening voice: 'What is this noise? Is it up to you to talk or up to us?' They all stopped immediately, they said no more, and all the animals were silent. When the master got up, he went to the lake and made a sign which meant: 'From now on you are allowed to speak.' Immediately, all the frogs went back to croaking." (Aflâkî *Manâqib ul-'Arifîn,* I, 134)

One day Rûmî asked a young disciple to get a large quantity of sweets. Rûmî then took the plate, covered it with a napkin and left. "I walked very discreetly behind him," the narrator tells us, "and he went to some ruins where I saw that a bitch had just given birth. The master gave all the provisions to the dog for her nourishment. I was flabbergasted by this compassion and this pity. 'It has been a week,' he told me, 'since this poor being has had anything to eat. She cannot leave because of her small ones. God has transmitted her complaints to me and ordered me to console her.'" (Aflâkî, *ibid.,* p. 294)

Once he was preaching the mystic precepts among all the citizens of Konya who had assembled in the market place. At the moment of the evening prayer, the dogs formed a circle around him. He was continually glancing toward them and going on with his explanations. They were wagging their tails and were growling happily. He said: "I swear by God, the Lord Almighty, that these dogs understand our gnosis." And he recited: "This door and this wall proclaim the praise of God and understand the Divine Secrets! The door and the wall tell subtle things, the fire, the water and the earth all tell their tales." (Aflâkî, *op. cit.,* I, 171)

This compassion and kindness were extended to all beings, especially the weakest; however, they did not exclude a solid common sense, great finesse and a great sense of humor. To someone who was telling him: "Last night I read the whole Koran, for the love of you," he answered: "And you did not die from it?"

His great tenderness is also revealed in this story: "One day a friend was hammering a nail into the wall of one of the college's cells. 'This cell,' he said, 'was our master's, Shams-od-Dîn's. Aren't you afraid of putting a nail into it? Let no one do it any more. I have the impression that one is putting the nail into my heart.'" (Aflâkî, *op. cit.,* II, 23) He had, on the other hand, a very earthly understanding of common events and a forthrightness which reminds one of tales of the Middle Ages. For Rûmî, anything that could seem trivial was, on the contrary, a means for him to make people perceive reality. "My tricks," he used to say, "are no jokes at all. They are a teaching. They are meant to direct and make my thoughts understood." (Aflâkî, *op. cit.,* I, 293)

His light humor colored everything he touched with an inimitable flavor. He could not stand sectarianism and the narrowness of mind of the righteous doctors of the Law, with their legality without love. He liked to repeat: "If you are searching, search with joy, for We inhabit the kingdom of joy." (Aflâkî, *op. cit.,* I, 276)

Neither Mawlânâ nor his disciples differentiated between religions, and anyone could become part of his entourage. After the death of his first wife, who had left two small infants, Djalâl-od-Dîn married a Christian woman, Kirâ-Khatûn of Konya, who had converted to Islam. He was loved by the Christian community as well as by the disciples of the other religions. His tolerance also extended to the non-believers. "The whole world," he said, "is made of parts of one single individual, which is represented by this tradition of the Prophet: 'O Lord, direct my people for they do not know!' My people, i.e., my constituent parts, for if the non-believers were not part of it, my people would not be the whole." (Aflâkî, *op. cit.,* I, 126)

He loved to quote Sanâ'i: "Atheism and faith run together on the Lord's path." He would put the accent on the oneness of the goal that all beings want to achieve. "There are many ways to search but the object of the search is always the same. Don't you see that the roads to Mecca are all different, one coming from Byzantium, the other from Syria, others running through land or sea? The roads are diverse, the goal, one . . . When the people arrive there, all quarrels, disputes or differences that occurred on the road are resolved. Those who were saying to each other on the road, 'You are wrong,' or 'You are an infidel,' forget their differences when they arrive because there the hearts are in unison." (*The Book of Inner Knowledge,* ch. 23)

Mawlânâ Djalâl-od-Dîn spent the rest of his life in Konya, composing an immense work and dispensing his spiritual teaching to many correspondents, friends and diciples. The latter would assemble within the brotherhood, or *tarîqa,* that he had founded and which was forever marked with his personal traits: humanity, fraternity, humility and tolerance.

The *tarîqa,* brotherhood of the whirling dervishes

Tarîqa, an Arabic term meaning "path, road, way," has had two meanings in Islamic mysticism.[1] At first the word designated a method of moral psychology to guide each individual, setting an itinerary for the soul's travel toward God, leading it through several stages, from the literal observance of the Law (*Sharî'a*) to the Divine Reality (*Haqîqa*). It held this meaning through the 9th and 10th centuries. The names of the great sufis, Djonayd, Hallâdj, Sarrâdj, Qûshayrî and Hudjwîrî are associated with this meaning.

At the beginning of the 11th century, the term *tarîqa* came to designate the group of rites of spiritual training necessary for the communal life of the different Islamic congregations that were being founded at that time. By extension it became synonymous with brotherhood and therefore refers to a community founded on special prescriptions under the authority of a single master.

Membership in one of these brotherhoods required that one reside in a "monastery" (*takya*) for varying periods of time. The *murîds,* or disciples very rarely stayed permanently; most of them were married and led normal outside lives. In this way the brotherhoods resembled the Christian Third Orders.

The *tarîqa* Mawlawîya was founded in Turkey by Djalâl-od-Dîn Rûmî, but it was his eldest son, Sultân Walad, who became its real organizer. The most original custom of that *tarîqa* is the celebrated dance, the *samâ',* which gave the members the name of the whirling dervishes. Every member of the brotherhood, in principle, has to follow certain prescriptions of meditation, prayers, etc., and must attend the regular meetings of his *tarîqa.*

Rûmî: his oldest portrait (Municipal Museum of Istanbul).   35

The treatises of Sufism describe very precisely the Rule followed in each *takya,* as well as the stages (*maqamât*) crossed by the pilgrim (*sâlik*). The role of the sheikh, or *murshid,* who directs the murîds, and to whom is due an absolute obedience, consists of adapting the exercises to the spiritual needs and possibilities of the disciples. The links between master and disciple are much more binding than those connecting a student to a mentor. This is not only the teaching of a method, conforming to the aptitudes of men aspiring to a spiritual life, but it is an initiatic transmission, the communication of a spiritual influence, a divine influx (*baraka*), that can only be given by a representative of a "chain" (*silsila*) going back to the Prophet himself. This initiation is symbolized by the investiture, the acceptance of the frock (*khirqa*).

The *murîd* is called the son of the sheikh and the disciples themselves consider each other as brothers. They love each other for the love of God and are united by a spiritual affinity stronger than blood. Thus, the sufi community constitutes an indivisible fraternity, the most recent adept feels spiritually linked to the most exalted hierophant. The bond between them can never be broken, for it is a marriage of souls that has been sealed in heaven.[2] Thus, says Abû-Sa'îd ibn Abi-l Khayr, a famous Persian sufi master: "Although one is in the East and the other is in the West, they find comfort and joy in each other's conversations and the one who lives a generation after his friend still finds guidance and solace in his words."

Abû-Sa'îd ibn Abi-l Khayr was the first to put a monastic prescription down in writing for the residents of his *takya* to follow. They are of great interest to us because they precede the foundation of the Mawlawîya by two centuries and constitute a typical Rule.

I. Let them keep their habits clean and themselves always pure.

II. Let them not talk inside the mosque or in any other sacred place.

III. Let them accomplish their prayers in common.

IV. Let them devote much time to the nocturnal prayers.

V. At dawn let them ask their Lord's forgiveness and invoke His name.

VI. Let them read as much of the Koran as they can during the morning and let them not speak before sunrise.

vii. Between the sunset prayers and the evening prayers they should recite litanies.

VIII. Let them welcome the poor and the needy and bear with patience the task of serving them.

IX. Let them eat nothing unless they share it with each other.

X. Let them not leave the monastery without asking permission from one another.

In addition, they should devote their spare time to the study of theology, the exercise of devotion or the consolation of others.

THE ASCETIC PRACTICES OF THE TARIQA MAWLAWIYA

The Retreat (tchella)

The retreat, or stay in the monastery, in Islam was generally 40 days. But the Mawlawî dervish had to retreat for a thousand and one days, not leaving his *takya* without permission. Any infraction meant that he had to start all over again. Therefore, for three years the Mawlawî disciple had to lead a very austere life. In the other "orders," the sheikh gave the *murîd,* according to his spiritual "state," one of the names of God, on which he was to meditate during the *dhikr* (recital of God's names). But at the Mawlawî order, the novitiate was given difficult and tiring tasks to perform, such as sweeping the floor, cleaning the baths and repairing the dervishes' shoes. He was to accomplish these tasks faithfully, readily and obediently, always saying "thank Thee to God," and showing great respect for those who preceded him in the brotherhood. The *tchella kash,* as the novitiate was called, worked all day and rested only after the evening prayer. He slept in a cell by himself without a mattress or blanket, only covering himself with his coat when it was very cold. There was always an old man among the dervishes called *meydan-djé,* who would take care of their cells and wake them up an hour before sunrise and light the candles in the mosque. After the *adhân,* the call to prayer, prayers were recited in common.

When a novitiate, during his retreat, made a mistake or was disrespectful to his superiors, the sheikh would punish him in front of all the dervishes assembled by flogging him 10 or 20 times on his legs.

The frugal meals were taken in common around a piece of leather on the floor that served as a table. The dervishes ate from the same plate and in a rather uncomfortable position, sitting and slightly reclining, which deterred any desire to eat too much.

Contrary to many masters, Rûmî forbade his disciples to beg. He reminded them that the Prophet had said one day: "One should keep his honor, one should work." He added: "Everyone is capable of working for his living. One can trade, another can be a scribe. He who does not behave in this way has no right to a dime." (Aflâkî, *op. cit.*, p. 219). The rule said that a mawlâwî dervish could not accept alms unless he had gone three days without eating.

Prayer and fasting

Far from advocating quietism or laxness in the religious observances, the Master prescribed that they should be performed rigorously. "All the prescriptions that the prophets and the saints have ordered or forbidden, all the solid constructions they have established, measuring them carefully, incite us to do the same. It is a duty to practice them, to perpetuate them and pledge to follow them." (Aflâkî, *op. cit.*, I, p. 150)

At the call of the muezzin, Rûmî would get up promptly and with profound respect he would say: "Let Thy Name live to Eternity, O Thou who lightens our heart."

His servant relates that during a very harsh winter in which the young men felt the cold, in spite of wearing their thick pelisses by a chimney or an oven, the Master would get up to the terrace and spend all night praying and crying until dawn. When he came down after the morning prayer, the servant would take his boots off and see his feet bleeding. His companions cried." (Aflâkî, *op. cit.*, I, p. 151)

He exhausted himself with fasting, saying: "Rest, for a mystic lover is in exhaustion. He finds a treasure in hardship and joy in seeking." One day as Rûmî was in a public bath, he looked at himself with pity and said: "I have never felt embarrassed by anyone before except now that I see how much my body has become thin. I understand its language and what it is telling me about its situation, what it was hiding but expressing with these complaints: 'You are giving me no rest, not even one whole day or a whole night so that I can gather my strength and help you bear the burden.' What could I say? My peace of mind rests on the fatigue I impose on my body. Should I get one moment of peace, my soul would not." (Aflâkî, *op. cit.*, I, p. 309)

What, for a sufi, is the deep meaning of prayer? Mawlânâ was asked one day: "Is there a quicker way to God than praying?" He answered: "More prayer. But praying is not only this external form. This is the *body* of the prayer; the formal prayer has a beginning and an end, and anything that has a beginning and an end is a body. The *takbîr* (the proclamation of the greatness of God) is the beginning of the prayer and the *salâm* (saluting the world) is its end. Also the *shahâda* (proclaiming one's faith) is not only what is said with one's lips, for this formula has a

Konya: the mawlawî takya (16th c. miniature).

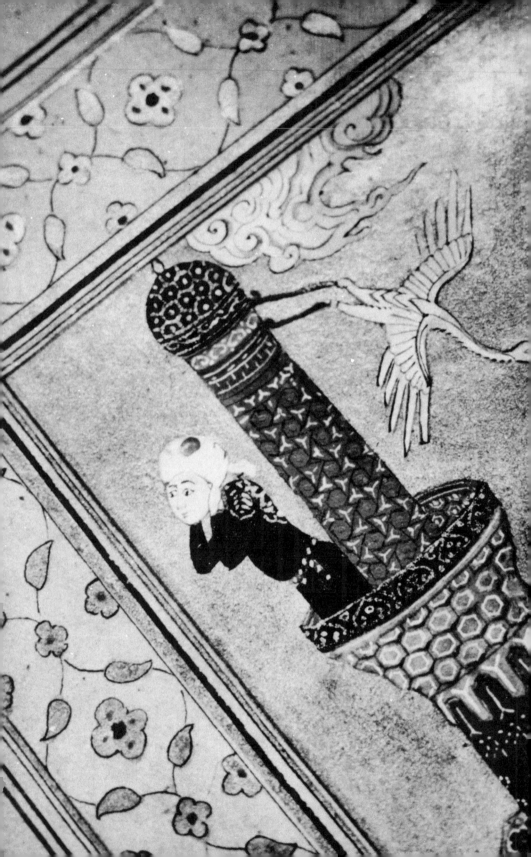

beginning and an end, and all that is expressed with letters and sounds and has a beginning and an end is a form and a body. But the soul of the prayer is unconditioned and infinite; it has no beginning nor end. The prophets (to them the salutation) brought us the prayer and the Prophet, who has taught it to us, said: "I have moments with God that no envoy nor angel has reached." Thus, the soul of the prayer is not only its form, it prepares one to be absorbed in God, and to lose consciousness. All the other forms remain exterior. Then, there is no place in the heart, even for Gabriel, who is a pure spirit." (*The Book of Inner Knowledge*)

THE TARIQA MAWLAWIYA IN HISTORY

The Mawlawîs were organized as a proper brotherhood by Sultân Walad. The first house, in Konya, became the center from which all the other *takyas* emanated. The master of the Mawlawya had the privilege, traditionally, of giving his sword to the Sultân when he took the throne. The successor of Sultân Walad, Tchelebi Amîr 'Adil gave his to Sultân Muhammad Fâtih, who became his disciple. From the 16th century on, the *takyas* were built by the emirs and the princes. Selim III (18th century), a sultân who was a poet and a musician, had an immense admiration for sheikh Ghalib, the Mawlawî poet, and composed all the music that we hear today for the *ney* (flute).

It was during this time that the *tarîqa* reached its apex. The *takyas* were repaired and the donations augmented. Often people joined the *tarîqa* to please the sultân. Many rulers favored the order, notably Mahmûd II (19th century) who had shut the Bekhtâshis convents and had severely repressed them. So the Bekhtâshis took refuge in the *takyas* of the Mawlawîs who gave them shelter.

At the beginning and throughout Rûmî's time, the order was completely decentralized. There was indeed the mother-house in Konya but there were *takyas* or branches of the *tarîqa* in the smallest villages. The Master was very close to the people without any embarrassment and had very little esteem for the mighty. His entourage was composed of artists, workmen and artisans. He always advised his followers to perform all kinds of work. The Mawlawîs, as we have said before, made no distinction between different sects and religions. They condemned fanaticism and encouraged the people to do so as well. Groups of dervishes traveled together and went to the humblest hamlets, earning their livelihood as they could, helping the population and performing the samâ' with them. Thanks to them, the poor would forget their misery. They also taught the *Mathnawî*. Even the women

The call to prayer.

41

took part in the concert, which was extremely revolutionary. The women did not have a *takya* but some of them had disciples, both men and women. Aflâkî tells us that the daughter of Sultân Walad, Sharaf Khâtûn, had several disciples and that a woman of Konya, 'Arifa Hoshlika, had very prominent men among her disciples.

During the 16th century the *tarîqa* changed. The order became centralized and was maintained through donations. The *awkafs* took it under their direction whereupon it lost its popular character, becoming more and more aristocratic and, thus, going contrary to the spirit of its founder.

At the beginning of the Ottoman period, the sultâns Murâd II (15th century) and Fâtih feared that the Mawlawîs would constitute a movement against them. During the revolt of Badr-ud-Dîn, his disciples were massacred but the Mawlawîs were not touched. The latter were sunni mystics, therefore orthodox, and did not meddle in politics. So from the 16th century on, the sultâns started to consider the Mawlawîs as a shield against the heretics and the revolutionary movements. From there came the growing favor they endured, and by the 18th century they had become a state institution. On the other hand, the shrinking of the empire closed many of the Mawlawî convents in Belgrad, Bosnia and in other regions outside of Asia Minor, and, little by little, even in Anatolia. The growing centralization accentuated its aristocratic character.

In 1925 Ataturk suppressed all the *tarîqas* in Turkey. The *takya* of Aleppo became the center for the remaining ones. There the dervishes were recruited and the sheikhs nominated, etc. The French government authorized its maintenance. In 1944, upon Syria's independence, the Syrian government refused to maintain the *takyas* and the Turkish *awkafs* took possession of their properties. Today, the old *takyas* have become museums, and the dues to visit them allow the old sheikhs to have a lifelong pension. There are still Mawlawî centers in Egypt, Cyprus and Libya.

THE INFLUENCE OF THE TARIQA MAWLAWIYA

The Ottoman Empire was immense, and the music, dance and poetry of the Mawlawîs were influential from Azerbaïdjan to Vienna. Amîr 'Arif Tchelebi, Djalâl-od-Dîn's grandson, traveled extensively, propagating his grandfather's doctrines. For centuries *takyas* were built in the farthest regions and the *Mathnawî* was read in various Turkish translations and commentaries so one did not need to read it in the original Persian. The princely families took great pleasure in the

Mawlawî poetry. Qâdi Burhân-od-Dîn, king of Siwas and also a poet, wrote praises of Rûmî. From the 15th century on, a whole Mawlawî literature ran parallel to the classical Turkish literature. Poets such as Ibrahim Beg, Sultân Dîwânî, Yusuf Sine Tchak, Arzi Dédé, Sheikh Ghâlib, Asrâr Dédé, Yeni Shehirli and Avni Beg are among the important ones related to this tradition. From the 16th century on, poets began to use Mawlawî terms. As early as the 15th century, Kamâl-od-Dîn Al-Khwârizmî al-Kubrâwî wrote a commentary on the *Mathnawî* in two volumes. We have translations in Turkish, Arabic and English as well as commentaries in Persian, Hindu and Turkish.

We do not know much about the Mawlawî music before the 17th century. Only three compositions dating from the 16th century or earlier have survived. We have two from the 17th century, nine from the 18th century, 26 from the 19th century and 20 from the 20th century. Mawlawî music, like the poetry, is extremely classical.

The artistic traditions of the *tarîqa* influenced the arts of painting and calligraphy. The museums of Konya contain some excellent examples of this, such as the first copy of the *Mathnawî,* ornate with gold and illuminations, written in the most beautiful calligraphy, and gilded embroideries covering the Master's tombs and those of his companions.

THE SAMA', COSMIC DANCE OF THE WHIRLING DERVISHES

Oh daylight, rise! atoms are dancing
The souls, lost in ecstasy, are dancing
To your ear, I will tell you where the dance will take you.
All the atoms in the air and in the desert,
Let it be known, are like madmen.
Each atom, happy or miserable,
Is in love with the Sun of which we can say nothing.

(Rubâ'iyât)

Thus, Djalâl-od-Dîn celebrated the cosmic dance. "There are many roads which lead to God," he would say, "I have chosen the one of dance and music." Every moment and every element of the *samâ',* this spiritual oratorio, has a symbolic meaning.

"One afternoon, a musician was playing the violin and the Master was listening with great pleasure. A friend entered and said, 'Stop this, they are announcing the afternoon prayer.' 'No,' said Djalâl-od-Dîn, 'this, also, is the afternoon prayer. They both talk to God. He wants the one externally for his service and the other for His Love and Knowledge." (Aflâkî, *op. cit.,* I, p. 309)

"A secret is hidden in the rhythms of music. Should I reveal it, it would upset the world." And he would add, talking about the *rebab:* "This is only a dry rod, a dry piece of wood and dry leather, but the voice of my Beloved rises from it."

When, at the sound of the *ney,* the dervishes thrust themselves whirling, it is the vertiginous trajectories of the planets that they want to enact as well as the universal movement.

The whole Cosmos reproduces a triumphal joy:

I see . . . the waters springing from their sources . . .
The branches of the trees are dancing like pilgrims,
The leaves flutter their hands like musicians.

(Mathnawî, IV, 3265-3268)

The ceremony of the *samâ'* is conducted in a very specific way. The dancers enter wearing white robes, symbols of the shroud, enveloped in ample black coats, representing the tomb, and coiffed with high felt hats, images of the tombstone. The sheikh, who represents the intermediary between the heavens and the earth, enters last. He salutes the dervishes and they return the gesture. He then sits in front of the red carpet whose color evokes the color of the setting sun which was illuminating the sky when Rûmî died on the 17th of December, 1273. The singer celebrates the praises of the Prophet *a capella* with a text written by Rûmî and music by the great Turkish composer Itri (end of the 17th century). "It is you, the beloved of God, the envoy of the sole Creator . . ." It is a slow and solemn composition. Then the flutist begins improvising while the master of the kettledrums plays them and the sheikh knocks on the ground. The dervishes then advance slowly and turn three times around the dance floor. The three rounds are symbolic of the three stages that take one nearer to God: the path of science, the path to the vision and the path leading to the union with God.

At the end of the third turn the sheikh takes his place on the carpet. The dervishes let their black coats fall, springing out of them wearing white as if liberated from their earthly envelope for a second birth. They ask the sheikh for permission to dance and then start whirling slowly, spreading their arms like wings, the right palm turned upward toward the sky to gather the divine grace, and the left palm turned downward to give it to the earth. This grace has crossed their hearts and has been warmed by their love. The movement they perform around the floor represents the universal law, the planets turning around the sun and around their own center. The drums evoke the trumpets of the last judgement. The circle of dancers is divided into two semi-circles, one represents the arc of the descent, or the involution of

The ney player (mawlawî calligraphy)

the souls into matter, and the other, the arc of the ascent of the soul toward God.

The Sheikh enters the dance at the fourth turn as the rhythm doubles in time, becoming very rapid. The sheikh turns at the center of the circle, he represents the sun and its rays. When he enters the dance the *ney* improvises again. This moment is the supreme moment of the achieved union. When the sheikh returns to his place, the *samâ'* is over and the singer recites the Koran; God's words answer the dervishes. Then the last salutations take place and God's name is evoked: *Hû* (Him). It is toward Him only that this adoration has ascended. "Anywhere you turn is the Hidden Face of Allah," says the Holy Book of Islam.

Rabindranath Tagore asked God to make him into a reed that He could fill with his music, and Rûmî likewise writes: "We are the flute, our music is from Thee . . ." (*Mathnawî*, I, 599). Commenting on this Islamic tradition: "The first thing God created was the *Kalâm* (the reed pen)." Rûmî relates that the Prophet had once told his son-in-law, 'Ali, mysteries that he had forbidden him to repeat. For 40 days, 'Ali tried to contain himself. Then, as he could not stand it any more, he went to the country, plunged his head into the mouth of a well and started to relate all these secrets. During his mystic drunkenness his saliva dropped into the well. A few days later a reed started to grow in it. It grew quickly day after day. A shepherd cut this reed, made a few holes in it and started to play it while keeping his sheep. His playing became famous; thousands came to hear him and cried with joy at the sound of his music. Even the camels made a circle around him. The story spread very quickly and came to the Prophet's ear who asked that the shepherd be brought to him. After a few preludes, everybody fell into ecstasy. "These melodies are the commentaries of the mysteries I told 'Ali," said the Prophet. "Thus, if someone among the seekers of purity is devoid of purity he cannot hear the mysteries contained in the melody of the flute, nor can he enjoy it, because faith is pleasure and passion."

"I asked the reed," says one of Rûmî's quatrains, "what is your complaint? How can you moan without a tongue?" The *ney* answered me: "I was separated from the sugar cane and I cannot live without lamenting and weeping."

Every *samâ'* starts with the famous prologue of the *Mathnawî* in which the *ney* is the symbol of the mystic's soul which laments because it is far from the spiritual world.

Listen to the reed flute telling you a story and lamenting the separation:
Since I was cut from the stalk, my song makes men and women weep.

I want a heart split by the separation to fill with the sorrow of
   my desire.
Whoever is far from his source, aspires to the moment when he will
   be reunited.
As for me, I complain constantly, both to those who are happy and to
   those who are crying.
Each one understands me according to his heart, but no one has tried
   to discover my secret.
My secret, though, is not very different from my complaint, but the ear
   and the eye cannot perceive it.
The body is not opaque to the soul, nor the soul to the body, still no one
   can see the soul.
It is fire, not wind, that is the sound of the flute: Let he who is missing
   this flame be destroyed!
The fire of Love is in the reed, the ardor of Love makes wine boil.
The flute is the confidant of the one who is separated from
   the Friend; its accents break our veils.

(Mathnawî, I, I s.)

For Djalâl-od-Dîn, the *samâ'* was not only a religious ceremony, it
was a spontaneous reaction, showing one's emotions, either joy or pain.
Sultân Walad tells us that after the death of his beloved master, Shams
of Tabrîz, which had plunged him into despair, his father would not
stop dancing.

Tradition explains thus, the *samâ'* that was done walking in the
streets: on their way home from the Friday prayers, the dervishes
played the *ney* and the *kudum* (drum) to express their joy.

It seems that any emotion, any strong impression would be enough to
incite the Master to dancing. There are famous examples in which a
sufi, upon hearing a word, would create a pun giving it a mystical
meaning. For instance, once on a feast day, in the middle of the bazaar
in Konya, a Turk was passing, holding a fox's fur and crying in a loud
voice: *Dilkou! Dilkou!* (fox). The Master gave a cry and started
dancing: "Where is the heart? (*Dil Kou*), Where is the heart?" and
danced all the way back to the college.

Another time, when Djalâl-od-Dîn was in the country, he went into a
mill and stayed there for a long time. His companions went searching
for him and, upon entering the mill, saw him performing the ritual
dance in front of the millstone. "In the name of God," he cried, "isn't it
true that this millstone is saying: 'Subbûh! Quddûs! (Oh Thee the
Glorious! The Holy!).'" Sheikh Sadr-od-Dîn, who was with him, went
on to say: "The Qadî Sirâdj-od-Dîn and I heard very clearly that these
words were indeed uttered by the millstone.

"The sufi turning around his center like the atom turning in the sun of eternity." (detail of a 16th c. miniature).

And the Master recited this *ghazal:*

The heart is like a grain of sand and we are the millstones;
does the millstone know why it turns?
The body is like the millstone, the thoughts are like
the water which makes it go round; the millstone talks and
the water knows what went on.

(Aflâkî, I, p. 291)
Manâqib ul-'Arifîn

We are told that one day the Master was passing in front of the shop of Salâh-od-Dîn Zarkûb, the gilder. The rhythm of the beaters reached his ears and he started whirling. The sheikh signaled the workers not to stop beating. The dance took place from the middle of the morning until the afternoon prayer. (Aflâkî, *op. cit.,* I, p. 336-337)

Let me extract this commentary written by a dervish of Konya in a personal letter to me: "The *ney* and the *Insân-ul-kâmil* (the man of God) are one and the same thing. Both lament their separation, both have been wounded in the chest, and both are bound. Both are dried because they are not nourished by the earth, and both are empty, filled only with the air of the musician. When they are alone, they have no voice. Their role is to be in the fingers and the mouth of the musician, to be his instrument so he can express his desire. The Man of God has been brought from the garden of pre-eternity of the divine world and falls by the force of destiny into the material world. He has been chained with the ropes of humanity and nature. His heart is wounded by the burn of the separation. He empties his heart of carnal desire and he empties his spirit of the imaginary existence and he abandons himself to God. He then is an instrument to express God's will, that is his only duty. When the Divine Voice wants to express itself, it borrows the different voices of each spiritual man.

"When the latter talks about the celestial origin and the sorrow of the separation, his listeners, if their hearts are pure, experience the same sadness. But there are many spiritual *degrees* in men and each man understands according to his *degree*. That is why our Master used to say 'Who has ever seen a poison and an antidote like the flute?' For some it expresses an earthly desire, a poison, while for others, it is the divine memory which it manifests . . .

"The *ney* is like a friend or a lover. First the lovers are separated and their faces veiled. Thus is the flute hidden in the pouch and suspended, but the *ney* is made to sing, and only then do we understand its secrets."

THE SYMBOLISM OF THE SAMA'

A great classical Turkish poet, Dîvâne Mehmed Tchelebi, in his *Treatise on the Mawlawî Meetings,* explains the symbolism of the *samâ'* in this way:

It happened that a King said to a dervish: "What is this frock
and what is this bonnet on your head?"
The dervish answered: "Oh most illustrious King, the frock is
my tomb and the bonnet is my tombstone."
The King said: "How is it that a dead person can talk, oh Father?
No one has heard this in this world before."
The other answered: "Have you not heard, oh King, that there is
an interrogation in the tomb and that one has to answer?"
The other said: "Does the dead man dance in this world? Who is
the one who prepares his place for dancing?"
The other said: "At the very moment that the trumpet blasts, the
dead will rise to dance."
The other said: "What is the secret of the whirling dance of
the Mawlawîs, oh my friend?"
The other said: "When it comes to his secrets, this would be
enough: you have to go back to where you came from."
He went on to say: "It is the secret of the origin and of the
return. Only our Master can explain it."

The other said: "Answer me, what is the secret of the Master who is like the sun in his Sign?"
The other said: "Listen to me, oh King of the world, I will speak to you and expose his secret.
"Before the world was created, when no creature or man existed, God was a hidden treasure, nothing but He existed, oh King.
With Him there were only names and attributes. What was other than Him was void in its essence.
He wanted to be known with His Attributes, and gave an order, creating the universe, with the letters *Kâf* and Nûn.[3]
"He made for himself, a mirror, oh King, and God saw himself with His Attributes.
"Man is this mirror of God, look at it with intelligence; the One who is seen is God, His Names and His Attributes.
"We could say that this pure essence is a point, it is from the speed of its evolution that all possibility comes.
"Inside that imaginary circle, the beings evolve as well as the men and the *genii* and all that is potential.
"Know that the circle has two different faces, put the one on the right and the other on the left.
"The right face is the external world, the left face is the internal world.
"Facing Him, is the place of man. Man is the mirror of the Compassionate.
"The point evolves along the imaginary circle, it turns, coming back on itself.
"When the point comes back to its point of departure all branches disappear on their own.
"Anything which is not God, the potential beings, we could say, are a point.
"They evolve along the imaginary circle like science evolves into knowledge.
"When the potentials come back to their origin, anything which is not God disappears; all that remains is His pure Essence.
"At that moment God reveals Himself to His servants with the name Peace.
"Let Peace be with you, oh My servants, you are now liberated from doubts and hesitations.
"You have known My Unity with certitude, Peace be on you, oh believers.
"Listen to the secret of the second circle, I will tell you the secret of the dance.
"The lovers turn a second time until they disappear like the science did.
"The Master of men reveals Himself and says: 'Let Peace be on you, oh lovers!
'You have known My Unity through your own experience, for I am perceived and perceive with certitude.'

"Listen to the secret of the third turn, Oh Noble man! The lovers call it *absolute Truth*.
"They also call it *complete annihilation* and *death, complete disappearance* and *death*.
"After which, God said, with the name of Peace: 'Peace be on you, oh lovers!
'In dying you have liberated yourselves from death. By the annihilation you have found again, the path toward Me.'
"The sheikh who is the vicar of God and whose being is the absolute void,
"This vicar is the interpreter of God, it is in God's language that he pronounces the three salutations.
"That state is the secret of the *qâb qawsain*[4], as Mawla Djalâl has shown.
"His sainthood, Mawlâ-i-Rûm Shams-i-Dîn, exposed thus the absolute mysteries.
"Having heard this, oh King of the world, that the path of the Friends and lovers
"Contains many secrets and mysteries that the Friends alone can know,
"Know then that in consequence, the one whose soul is never in opposition with the Friends is happy, but the one who, having seen them, denies the evident secrets, is a miserable man who resembles a bat,
"Do not attach yourself to the appearances of this world for with this eye, you can never see a correct path.
"With the light of Shams, of Djalâl-od-Dîn Rûmî, these sciences are clearer than the day and the moon.
"The dervishes are like the stars which guide you in the path of Djalâl-od-Dîn Rûmî.
"Compared with his light, the sun is only an atom — this man is more luminous than the world."
(M. Molé, The Sacred Dances, 'Oriental Sources', p. 248 s.)

The ceremonies of the *samâ'* did not go without arousing controversy and we can find the echo of it in the chronicles which relate the objections formulated by the "righteous" elements of Konya against Mawlânâ. Orthodox Islam is suspicious of listening to music as a technique for ecstasy. The Koran condemns praying in a drunken state, and the soul can get drunk with harmony and dance as well as with wine, or more subtly still, from its own spiritual *state*. The great masters of sufism have always warned their disciples very carefully against false mysticism whose goal is the evasion of the self. No one has condemned this more severely than Djalâl-od-Dîn Rûmî, who hated any spiritual sensuality with a rigor equal to that of St. John of the Cross. One should not forget the forcefulness with which he recommended not to be in love with Love but with the Beloved. At a certain signal in the Mawlawî dance, the dervish must instantly stop his whirling. This insures the opportunity of cutting short any state capable of annihilating the lucidity of the dancer.

The spiritual concert is justified as a means to illuminate consciousness; the music is an awakening of the soul. It makes the soul remember a forgotten homeland. For Plato and the neo-platonitians, all knowledge is but a reminiscence. Jamblique remarks that certain airs of music can establish a communication with the divine, as the soul finds in them, the echo of the eternal musics it heard on other planes. The Koran does talk about the pre-eternal pact made between God and Adam's race (VII, 172). It is to this pact that the great mystic Djonayd attaches the deep significance of the *samâ'*. He was asked once why the sufis shook in ecstasy while listening to the music. He answered: "When God interrogated the genes in Adam's kidneys during the primordial pact, saying: 'Am I not your Lord?' a gentleness was implanted in the souls. When they hear music, this memory awakens and shakes them."

This is the meaning of the admirable passage in the *Mathnawî* in which Djalâl-od-Dîn Rûmî relates the conversion to sufism of Ibrahîm ibn Adham, who abandoned his kingdom. He was listening to his musicians during the night:

His goal, while listening to the sounds of the rebeck, was, as
is the case with the fervent lovers of God, to remember the
Divine Word,
For the pointed sound of the bugle and the menace of the drums
somewhat resembled the universal trumpet.
That's why the philosophers said that we receive these harmonies
from the revolution of the celestial sphere
And that the melody that the people sing accompanied by the
pandora is the sound of the revolutions of the sphere.
The real believers say that the influence of Paradise has made
every unpleasant sound splendid.
We are all part of Adam, we have heard these melodies in
Paradise.
Although the water and the clay (of our bodies) have placed
us in doubt, something of these melodies comes back to our
memory.
Mixed as they are with this earth of affliction, how could these
sounds, high pitched or somber, give us the same delight? . . .
That is why the *samâ'* is the food of the lovers of God for it
contains the image of peace.

(*Mathnawî*, IV, 731 s.)

The *samâ'* is peace for the souls of the living,
The one who knows this, possesses peace in his heart.
The one who wants to be awakened,
Is the one who sleeps in the middle of the garden.
But for the one who sleeps in prison,
To be awakened is only a nuisance.
Go to the *samâ'* while a wedding is being celebrated,
Not during a funeral or in a place of lamentation.
The one who does not know his own essence
The one from whom is hidden this beauty similar to the moon,
What would such a person do with the *samâ'* or the drums?
The *samâ'* is made for the union with the Beloved.
Those who have their faces turned toward the *Qibla,*
For them it is the *samâ'* of this world and the other.
Even more for the circle of dancers within the *samâ'*
Who turn and have in their midst, their own *Ka'aba.*

(*Mystic Odes, 339*)

Rûmî's Death

"The Wedding Night" (sheb-el-arus), as it is commonly called, was the 17th of December, a well-known date to everyone in Turkey. The day commemorates the departure for eternal life of the one who, all his life, aspired toward the supreme meeting. During his last illness, he said to a friend who had come to wish him a prompt recovery:

> "When between the lover and the Beloved there is only a poor shirt left, wouldn't you want the light to unite with the Light?"

And he recited,

> How should I be afflicted, when every part of my being is blooming?
> Why shouldn't I go out of this well? Don't I have a solid rope?
> I have built a penthouse for the pigeons of the soul.
> Oh bird of my soul! Fly away, for I possess a hundred fortified towers.
>
> (Aflâkî, *op. cit.,* II, p. 89)

Had he not, for a long time, warned those who would be tempted to surrender to grief:

> When on the day of my death, they will carry my coffin,
> Don't think that my heart has remained in this world.
> Don't cry over me, don't say: "Tragedy, tragedy!"
> You would be falling into the trap of the demon, that would be
> a tragedy.
> When seeing my corpse, don't exclaim: "Gone, gone!"
> The union and the meeting will be mine then.
> When you entrust me to the tomb, don't say: "Adieu, adieu!"
> For the tomb hides the union in Paradise from us.
> You saw the decline; find the elevation.
> For the moon, for the sun, is their setting harmful?
> To you it looks like a sunset; in fact, it is a dawn.

Konya: Rûmî's tomb.

Does the tomb look like a prison to you? It is the liberation
of the soul.
What grain sown in this earth has not germinated one day?
Why doubt? Man is also a buried grain.
What bucket has gone down empty and has not come back up full?
The spirit is like Joseph; would he complain about the well?
Keep silent here and talk in the other world
So that your song of victory will resonate beyond space.

(Mystic Odes, 911)

When what Rûmî had called the *dawn of death* (*Mathnawî*, IV, 3628)
arrived, all the citizens of Konya, regardless of their faith, took to
mourning. Aflâkî describes the funeral:

"After they had brought the corpse on a shaft, the totality of the
people, rich and poor alike, uncovered their heads. Women, men and
children, everyone was there. There was an uproar so loud that it could
have been the day of the great Resurrection. Everyone was crying and
most of the men were walking and wailing, tearing their robes, their
bodies bare. The members of all communities and cultures were present:
Christians, Jews, Greeks, Arabs, Turks, etc. They walked in front, each
holding high their Holy Book. Each was reading the Psalms, the Penta-
teuch or the Gospels, according to their faith. The hurling and lamenting
was so great that the Moslems could not have held them back with canes
or swords. The thunderous tumult was soon heard by the sultan and his
minister Pervané who sent for the leaders of these denominations and
asked them why they were so affected when the one they were mourning
was the imam of the Moslems. They answered: 'When we saw him, we
understood the real nature of Christ, of Moses and of all the prophets.
We have found, in him, the perfect conduct described in our Books as
being the conduct of the perfect prophets. Just as you Moslems claim that
Mawlânâ was the Mohammad of our time, so we think that he is the
Moses and the Jesus of our time, and just as you are his faithful friends,
so are we, and a thousand times more, his servants and disciples. Had he
not said: '72 sects will hear from us, their own mystery. We are like the
flute, which, with a single mode, is tuned to 200 religions.'

'Our Master is the sun of the truths which has shone on all mortals and
given them his favors. Everyone loves the sun which lights everyone's
house.'

"Another Greek priest said, 'Mawlânâ is like the bread which is indis-
pensible to all. Has anyone seen a hungry man run away from bread?
And you, how do you know who he was?' All the lords fell into silence.
In the meantime, the readers of the Koran, with their gentle pronuncia-
tion, were reciting the marvelous verses. It was a painful and somber
moment; the muezzins, with their clear voices, chanted the prayer of

Resurrection and twenty groups of master singers recited the funeral songs that our Master had written himself." (Aflâkî, *op. cit.,* II, p. 97)

Since that day, the anniversary of Rûmî's death is celebrated in Konya with solemn ceremonies. A *samâ',* the spiritual oratorio, is held in memory of the one who, himself, had said:

The King of pure thought
Dancing, has gone
To the other country,
The country of the Light.

Rûmî had said: "If you are seeking, seek Us with joy for We live in the realm of joy." So death itself should be a reason for rejoicing. One day his servant told him: "All the prophets and even the privileged people have trembled with fear in front of death and its torments." The Master answered: "God preserve us from such a feeling! Do men know what death is? Death, for the mystics, is to see the Supreme Truth. Why would anyone run away from that view?" (Aflâkî, *op. cit.,* I, p. 242)

". . . Those who recite the Holy Book, who walk in front of the funerals, testify that the deceased was a real believer, a Moslem and a mystic, and also that the human spirit which had been imprisoned for years within the prison of this world, and which had been kept prisoner of its tight body, has at last been delivered by God's grace and has reached thus its primeval center. Is this not a reason for rejoicing, for singing and praise? In manifesting one's joy in this way, one shows how much one wants to go back to the Glorious Lord and incite others to live their lives audaciously, for if, on earth, one was actually delivered from prison and covered with honors, wouldn't that provoke gratefulness and joy? Indeed the death of our friends is according to what has been said:

When they broke their chains it was a moment of joy.
They ran toward the fountain of happiness, they rejected the
ropes and chains.
The royal soul has sprung out of its prison, why should we
lament?

(Aflâkî, *op. cit.,* p. 213)

Arise, friends, let us go. It is time to leave this world.
The drum is beating in heaven, now he is calling us.
Look: the camel-driver has risen, he has prepared the caravan
And wants to go on. Oh travelers, why sleep?
In front of us, behind us, is the tinkling of the bells,
the tumult of departure.
At every moment, a soul, a spirit, flys away from here which
is no longer its place.

From the light of the stars, from the blue vault of heaven,
Mysterious figures have appeared, which are revealing the
secret things.
A heavy sleep has fallen on you from the whirling spheres.
Beware of this ephemeral life, beware of this heavy sleep.
Oh soul, look for the Beloved, oh friend, look for the Friend.
Oh you who watch the night, be on your guard; it is not good
for a watchman to sleep.

(Diwân-e Shams-e Tabrîzî)

Our death is our wedding with eternity.
What is the secret? "God is One."
The sunlight splits when entering the windows of the house.
When those windows are closed the multiplicity disappears.
This multiplicity exists in the cluster of grapes;
It is not in the juice made from the grapes.
For he who is living in the Light of God,
The death of the carnal soul is a blessing.
Regarding him, say neither bad nor good,
For he is gone beyond the good and the bad.
Fix your eyes on God and do not talk about what is invisible,
So that he may place another look in your eyes.
It is in the vision of the physical eyes
That no invisible or secret thing exists.
But when the eye is turned toward the Light of God
What thing could remain hidden under such a Light?
Although all lights emanate from the Divine Light
Don't call all these lights "the Light of God";
It is the eternal Light which is the Light of God,
The ephemeral light is an attribute of the body and the flesh.
. . . Oh God who gives the grace of vision!
The bird of vision is flying towards You with the wings of desire.

(Mystic Odes, 833)

Konya: The mausoleum of Mawlânâ Djalâl-od-Dîn Rûmî.

ASIA MINOR
&
SYRIA
About 1140

Konya,
The City of Saints

Made holy by the presence of Rûmî, a center of pilgrimage whose prodigious radiance is still active, Konya is one of those places which seem marked since the beginning of time for an extraordinary destiny.

Konya was, according to the Phrygians, the first city to emerge from the flood. Inhabited since the 6th millenium, it is a neighbor of what we consider today to have been the first urban community, Catal-Hüyük. Nine thousand years ago, that city had a very advanced civilization based on the great Anatolian myth of the Mother-goddess, who later was worshipped under the names of Artemis, Cybele and Diana.

An important city of the mysterious Hittite Empire, which is just starting to give some hint of its secrets, Konya saw the marriage of one of Ramses II's daughters. A capital during the Roman Empire, it was called Iconium in the times of St. Paul. Paul, the apostle Barnabus and his disciple Timothy (who was from Konya) taught the gospel there. Paul met the apostle Luke, by chance, along the road just outside of Konya. This region saw the birth of the first Christian communities and the meetings of the first synods. Byzantium's neighbor and her rival, it was crossed by the Crusaders. Afterward, it became the capital of the Seldjukide Empire of Roum, Anatolia.

Eleven civilizations succeeded each other in Konya. It was a cross-road for armies, a meeting place of East and West, the Greek World and the Asian; it was a land of archetypes, of scientists, of philosophers and saints. Anatolia played a considerable role in history. The great stature of Rûmî, who took its name for his own, is the living symbol of these values. He represents, not syncretism, but synthesis. He was the apostle of oecumenical thought in its most fraternal aspect.

The fact that his message was delivered in an epoch of torments, in a region of the world ravaged by wars, makes it all the more important.

He put himself higher than the quarrels; he demonstrated how vain they were.

Since Constantine, the Empire had been cut into two. Lamartine writes, in his *History of Turkey:* "In transplanting his empire from Rome to Byzantium, Constantine had not only changed his religion and his capital . . . The Emperor and the Oriental Romans kept from the Italian Romans only the pride and the despotism. The same voices were running into different bloodstreams. Luxury and licentiousness had, from reign to reign, weakened the characters . . ."

The Empire's government, venal and weak, encouraged the invasions. Attila's hordes, the Bulgarians, the Goths and the Norman adventurers came, like the Turks, to the doors of Constantinople. The Byzantines set their boats on fire.

In front of what was left of the Roman Empire, came new peoples with new and younger blood. The day was not far off when the Byzantine power would collapse to give way to the new power, the Seldjukide's, and it was the kingdom of Konya that would become the cradle of the Ottoman Turkey.

This dynasty started with Seldjuk, who belonged to a nomad tribe settled on the frontier of Afghanistan. He became a Moslem with the rest of his people and entered Transoxania in 689 and Islamized Central Asia. One of his descendants, Alp Arslan (1063–1072), reconquered the holy cities of Mecca and Medina from the hands of the Fatimides and expanded his kingdom from Afghanistan to Egypt. In 1067, he vanquished the Byzantine armies and entered Konya the following year. His son, Malik Shah, continued his conquests, taking Khorassan, Syria, Persia and Anatolia. After the first Crusade, Konya became the capital of the Seldjukide Empire and remained thus until its end.

When Djalâl-od-Dîn arrived there, the Seldjukide Kingdom was experiencing great prosperity. Its stability was founded on a strong and disciplined army, a loyal and efficient administration and a flourishing commerce. Agriculture had been highly developed and the provincial cities along the roads protected by the Seldjukides were prospering. The future looked bright for Sultân 'Ala-od-Dîn Kaykobâd I (1219–1236). He was the one, as we have said earlier, who had given hospitality to Rûmî's father and his family. He was a pious and wise man. His armies were victorious and Konya knew a period of glory. When he died, he left his son an empire that comprised all of Asia Minor. However, a few years later, in 1243, the Mongols, who in 1220 had destroyed the native city of Rûmî, won over the Seldjukides in the battle of Kozadag, a victory which changed the history of that region forever. The Seldjukides became the Mongols' vassals.

The history of this period is a long and continuous chain of struggle and intrigue. In fact, the Minister Mu'in-od-Dîn Pervané had the power and the sultân was only a figurehead. He was a wise and clever ruler, and gathered scientists and artists around him. He had very close relations with Rûmî and the *Book of Inner Knowledge* relates the numerous talks they had with each other. The Master wrote him several letters giving him wise advice.

From 1276–1277, three years after Rûmî's death, the Sultân of Egypt invaded Asia Minor and the Seldjukide and Mongolian armies were defeated. Although the Egyptians retreated, Mu'in-od-Dîn was accused of treason, condemned to death and executed by the Mongols on the 2nd of August 1277. The western chronicles tell us "he was cut by the middle."

Thus the Seldjukide splendor was extinguished almost at the same time as the Master. From then on Konya would shine only with his radiance. In 1308, the last Seldjukide sultân was put to death by the Mongols, and Osman, who, a quarter of a century earlier had been a captain (the Protector of the Border), rose to start the Ottoman dynasty.

In Rûmî's time, Konya was famous for its beauty. Barbarossa's Crusaders described it as being as big as Cologne, with a wall and a citadel. Rûmî himself described it thus: "In Konya, the leaders and the lords and the dignitaries have thousands of houses, castles and palaces. The merchants and the *ikdish* (bourgeois) have houses more magnificent than those of the artisans, the palaces of the emirs are more magnificent than those of the merchants and the domes and the palaces of the sultâns are more magnificent than all the others."

The Seldjukide sultâns were usually patrons of the arts and led a luxurious and refined life. As a whole, they were pious men and built many splendid mosques and *medresses* (schools). Thanks to Rûmî and his brotherhood, Konya was a center of immense religious fervor and has remained that way. A great tolerance reigned in it, so much so that in the 12th century, Theodore Balsamon wrote that it was better to be the subject of the Turks, who respected the souls of men, than of the Franks who threatened them.

One cannot say enough about the amicable relations Rûmî had with the Christians of Konya. Aflâkî relates: "In the monastery called Plato's monastery, there was a wise monk, very learned and very old. He told me that Rûmî once made a retreat of 40 days in his monastery. He had asked how Islam was superior to Christianity, as both religions were promising hell's fire to their sinners. The Master went to a bakery, took the monk's silk frock, wrapped it with his own and threw them into the oven. After a few moments they took both mantles out; the monk's was totally burnt and Rûmî's had been cleaned! That monastery was itself a place of pilgrimage for both Christians and Moslems. St. Amphilochius's church in Konya, which had been transformed into a mosque, was also revered by both communities until the 15th century, for the tradition held that the "Divine Plato" was buried there.

More significant still, is the legend that tells of a tomb next to Mawlânâ's in the *takya* of Konya. It is that of a Christian who had been such a close friend of his that he had demanded that he be buried next to him. The Armenians claim that he was a bishop named Eusébius, and the Greeks claim that he was the monk that we referred to above. The Mawlawîs claim that it is the tomb of a Christian monk who converted to Islam, thanks to Mawlânâ. It could also be a cenotaph elevated in the memory of a Christian friend. Whatever the case may be, the important thing is that it demonstrates that both communities were living together and sharing a fraternal spirit. The Seldjukide sultâns often married Christian women, who maintained the freedom to practice their religion, such liberties being a formal prescription of Islam. Therefore Rûmî could live in a climate that corresponded with his views and he contributed to their expansion. The traveler who comes today to pay homage to him at his tomb cannot but notice the serenity that emanates from it. It is as if everything there reflects his kindness.

Some of the monuments that Rûmî knew are still standing. Of 'Ala-od-Dîn Kaykobâd's palace, which was finished during Rûmî's time and is supposed to be the palace of Aladin of *The Thousand and One Nights,* only one wall remains today, but the beautiful mosque within the city's walls which bear Rûmî's name and where he preached, is still completely intact.

The admirable Karatay College is particularly interesting. Rûmî must have gone there to meditate and observe the sky, he who reflected so often on the constellations. A fountain, situated under the open center of the dome, allowed one to study the firmament and astronomy. A special installation, in the form of a treble cleff, drained the water in a way that left the surface smooth and still enough to reflect the stars as if in a mirror. Precious astrolabes are on display there. In many instances, Rûmî compares man to them, thus in the *Mathnawî:*

> Adam is the astrolabe of the attributes of the Divine Sublimity,
> the nature of Adam is a theater of the revelations of God.
> Everything that appears in him (man) is His reflection as the
> moon is reflected in the water of the river.
> The figures drawn on the tablet of this astrolabe are there to
> manifest the eternal attributes.

> (*Mathnawî,* IV, 3138)

But the heart of Konya is, of course, Djalâl-od-Dîn Rûmî's mausoleum. Under its cupola, a high turquoise dome covered with green tiles standing out from the blue azure of the sky, which seems to light the whole city with its radiance, rest Konya's Master and his family. A sumptuous coverlet, on which are embroidered Koranic verses with threads of gold, is placed on his coffin. The latter stands on a platform surrounded with a low railing in solid silver. Two silver steps lead to it which the pilgrims lean down and kiss. Next to him, his son, Sultân Walad is buried. On his left is his father's (Bahâ-od-Dîn's) coffin, standing upright. Tradition has it that he died standing up, as he had risen to welcome the prophet Mohammad who had come to assist him in his last moments. A little farther away are the tombs of other descendants. From the ceiling, which is ornate with magnificent sculptures, lamps shine in the semi-darkness. Richly illuminated manuscripts of the Koran and of the *Mathnawî,* robes having belonged to Mawlânâ and Shams of Tabrîz, musical instruments and old and precious Anatolian carpets from the 13th century also fill the room. An extraordinary peace reigns there.

On both sides of the square courtyard, are rows of cells surmounted with domes where the dervishes lived. They remind us that this was a monastery (*dergah*) until Mustapha Kemal abolished all the brotherhoods and it was turned into a museum. On the right are the refectory and the common room. Next to the latter is the *samâ'* room, where the dance was performed twice a month after the Friday prayer, and a library. The building's plan is the same as it was when the order was founded but it has been restored several times. On the pediment, one can read this verse written by the Master:

> Come, whoever you are, believer or unbeliever, come; here
> is the house of hope.

KONYA SAVED BY RUMI

"When Baïdjû's army attacked Konya and besieged the city, everyone despaired and started asking each other for shrouds. They came to the Master and asked him for his help. Mawlânâ . . . climbed on a hill which was situated behind the city's public place and performed the dawn prayer. Baïdjû's tent had been set up under that hill . . . They saw a person dressed in blue and coiffed with a grey turban standing on the hill and praying with perfect serenity while the world around him was in turmoil. At that time, the Mongol army ignored the enlightenment of Islam and the well-being of the faith. In many cities they had destroyed colleges, mosques and minarets. With perfect accord, the Mongols

At the Karatay College.

advanced and directed their arrows toward Mawlânâ, but their hands became tied and, in spite of all their efforts, they could not draw their bows. They mounted their horses and tried to climb the hill but no horse would advance. Meanwhile, all the inhabitants of the city were watching this manifestation of the Almighty from the towers, and were exclaiming *Allah-ou-Akbar* (God is great)!

"When Baïdjû heard the tale, he stood up, left his tent, and asked for his bow and arrows. He sent one in the direction of the Master, but the arrow, coming back on itself, fell into his army's ranks. Three times, he threw his horse up the hill and every time he had to admit that the horse would not move. Full of fury, he dismounted and walked, but his feet, tied by the power of the Almighty, could not move . . . Then Baïdjû, admitting the greatness of the miracle, said: 'From now on, let there be no war, nor combat.' The Mongol army lifted the siege and went to camp in the plains of Filoubad."

Baïdjû forgave the city. He asked its lords: "Who is this man? And where is he from?" They told him the story of Bahâ-od-Dîn Walad, from its beginning to its end.

Sultân Walad recounts: "My father used to tell us always: 'From now on give Konya the name of the City of Saints, for every child born in this town will be a saint. As long as the blessed body of Bahâ-od-Dîn and his descendants remain in this town, the town will be preserved from the sword. Its enemies will not succeed and, eventually, will perish. Konya will be secure against the horrors of the end of time. Even if part of it is ruined and erased, it will not be demolished totally, for, even ruined, our treasure would be hidden there." (Aflâkî, *op. cit.,* I, 230, 5)

That miracle took place in 654 (1256). Baïdjû contented himself with only dismantling Konya's walls, leaving those of the citadel which contained the burial grounds of the old sultâns.

سوار روش بون حکایت یکید
کریستان نامه آبریدهٔ آله
سبه خوام شرعه شرعه فزا
هر کسی کوده دیما دار نیلیش
من بهتر جمعتی تالار شدم
هر کسی ازطرحه خود شدیارین
شرمن ازاله مزد درنیش
تن زجان وجان فن مستور نیست
آشی ازاله می ویش باد

روزجدا یها شکایت ینکه
آدیعهم مرد ودن تن آله
تاکویم شرح درد اشیاق
بازجوم روزکار وصلی یرم
حقه جوش حالان ویقالان
وددردون مجنیا سه ردی
یلنجشم وکوثر آن بوشیت
لیلک کنر رادید دجاز دستور
هرکه ایر آتمه مدارد نیست باد

The Works of Rûmî

The principal work of Mawlânâ Djalâl-od-Dîn Rûmî is a vast poem of about 45,000 verses, divided into six books, the *Mathnawî*. The name comes from the special prosody employed, which consists of single lines divided into two rhyming phrases of 10 syllables each. Anecdotes, prophetic traditions, legends, folkloric themes and citations from the Koran follow each other, composing a mystic epic, "a majestic river, calm and deep, winding its way, between rich and varied scenery, into the unfathomable ocean." (Nicholson)

The lyrical part consists of the quatrains, *Rubâ'îyâts,* and the ghazals, or *Mystic Odes,* dedicated to his beloved Master Shams of Tabrîz, (*Diwân-e Shams-e-Tabrîz*). At the end of each poem, he cites his name. A complete edition was done by Professor Forûzânfar of Teheran. The beauty and power of these odes are beyond comparison.

His prose treatise, *Fîhi-mâ-fîhi,* which translates literally as "In it is what is there," has been published in French under the title, *"le Livre du Dedans,"* "The Book of Inner Knowledge." It is comprised of his sayings, taken down by his eldest son, Sultân Walad. The book is of considerable interest, not only for understanding the Master's thought, and sufism in general, but because of the depth and finesse of the analysis within it, which makes it an initiation in itself. Mawlânâ says, regarding it: "I have studied many sciences and have deployed much effort in order to offer the researchers and scientists who come to me, precious and rare knowledge. It is the Almighty God who has decided thus." (*The Book of Inner Knowledge*)

There are also letters addressed by Rûmî to various personalities in a volume titled *Maktûbât*. They give us valuable information about his private life and his epoch.

Madjâlis-e Sab'ah (The Seven Sessions) is a collection of public pre-
dictions that the Master gave and the *Khâbnâma* is a small pamphlet on
the interpretations of dreams.

The sources

Rûmî's sources for the themes and the anecdotes are varied. They
include Iranian folklore, the fables of *Kalîla-wa Dimna* and especially
the works of Sanâ'î and 'Attar. We find frequent allusions to Al Ghazâlî
and to his celebrated treatise on the revival of the religious sciences,
Ihyâ' 'Ulûm ud-Dîn, and to Avicenna and Nizâmi.

As for the doctrinal sources, excepting the Koran and the *hadîth,*
which were his natural nourishment, some came from the teachings of
Bahâ-od-Dîn Walad, his father, and some from Shams, who came later
and deeply influenced his thinking. Bahâ-od-Dîn's *Ma'ârif* was always
by his bedside and he must have meditated on Shams's *Maqalât* or
Maqâmât often.

Also, as we know, he had studied for several years in Aleppo and
Damascus, so he must have know 'Ibn ul-'Arabi's thought. He had met
his son-in-law, Sadr-od-Dîn Konyawî, with whom he would have discussed these teachings. But how much his doctrine owes to these
sources is difficult to say. The same problem arises regarding Plato,
whom he cites at the beginnig of the *Mathnawî.* He certainly had read
him and knew the neo-platonicians, but we can only estimate their role.

Rûmî was a spiritual master, a poet and a mystic, not a philosopher
or a logical theoretician. He had the possibility of drawing upon a rich
common knowledge. Byzantium was, at that time, a place of great culture where the Greeks were re-discovering their own thinkers through
the Arabic and Iranian translations. Konya, as we have seen, had an en-
lightened sultân who surrounded himself with scientists and artists. The
Islamic and Hellenistic currents intermingled in a fraternal climate of
exchange between Christians and Moslems. Furthermore, the main sufi
treatises had already been written. Therefore, if Rûmî's work had bene-
fited from these numerous sources and his thought enriched by them,
and, if he had found in his predecessors a conceptual mould which
received his individual experience, be it human or mystic, it is less
important than the power with which he transmitted his message, lyri-
cally and didactically. Sufism finds in him its most perfect form.

THE SPIRITUAL PATH: SUFISM

The Spiritual Path:
Sufism

The living heart of Islam (the actualization of the revelation), added to the faithful observance of the ritual practices, the *tarîqa* is designated by the word *Tasawwuf,* or sufism. It is the esoteric dimension of the Islamic message, which, like the *Sharî'a,* the religious Law, has its origin in the Koran and the prophetic tradition.

That sufism is fundamentally Islamic, whatever the more or less arbitrary affiliations attributed to it by the western orientalists may be — Vedanta, Christianity, Neo-Platonism — can in no way be doubted, for the spiritual realization is founded on the teachings of the Sacred Book, and Muhammad's practices.

The circle, as a geometric symbol, has been used sometimes to clearly show the link between the fundamental dimensions of Islam. The circumference represents the religious law which encompasses the whole Moslem community, the radius symbolizes the roads (*tarîqas*) which lead to the center where the Supreme Truth (*Haqîqa*) is found. This truth, being everywhere and nowhere, symbolically creates the *Tarîqa* and the *Sharî'a,* as a point creates the radius and the circumference at the same time. The Law and the Path, both brought into existence by God, who is the Truth, reflect the Center, each in its own way.[6]

Aspiring to join the center, ultimate goal of all quest and all love . . .
(Decorative motif in the mosque of Kerman, 16th c.)

The Path

"If you ask me, oh my brother, which are the signs of the Path, I would answer you very clearly and without ambiguity. The Path is to look at the truth and break with the falsity, it is to turn your face to the living universe, to despise the earthly dignities, to free your mind from any ambition of glory and fame, to stoop to His service, to purify your soul from evil and strengthen it with reason, to leave the house of those who talk too much and go to the one where people are silent and to travel from God's manifestations to God's Attributes and from there to His Knowledge. Then, at that moment, you will have crossed the world of mysteries and arrived at the door of Poverty. When you are Poverty's friend, your deep soul will have become a penitent heart. Then, God will extract Poverty from your heart, and when Poverty is gone from there, God will stay in your heart." (Sanâ'i, *Hadîqa*, p. 112–113)

For sufism, the notion of *Tawhîd,* that is, the Divine Oneness which is the essence of Islam, is not a different reality from the revealed religious Law (*as-Sharî'a*). They are both complemental aspects of that ultimate reality which constitutes the basis of the mystery of Being. As we read in the Koran, God is the External (*as-Zâhir*) and the Internal (*al-Bâtin*) at the same time. They manifest simultaneously "on the horizons and in the soul" (*Afâq wa anfûs*). Therefore there is no real sufism unless it is approached by two paths, obedience to the Law and the search for inner meanings (*al-ma'nâ'l-bâtinî*). This is explained in an old classical treatise, the *Risâlat* of Al-Qushairî:

"The *Sharî'a* deals with the observance of the rites and devotional acts, whereas the Truth (*Haqîqa*) is involved with the inner vision of the Divine Glory. Any devotion not filled with the spirit of Truth is worthless, and the spirit of Truth not structured by the Law is incomplete. The Law exists to govern humanity, and Truth makes us know the dispositions of God. The Law exists for the service of God, the Truth, for His contemplation. The Law exists for us to obey His prescriptions, whereas Truth makes us understand His commandments. One is external, the other is internal . . . Know that the Law is Truth because God has commanded it and Truth is also the Law because it is the knowing of God, which he has ordered as well." (*Ar-Risâlat al-qushairîya,* p. 43)

In the preface to the *Mathnawî's* fifth book, Rûmî insisted on the close links which join the Sacred Law (*Sharî'a*), the Path that the sufis should follow (*tarîqa*) and the Ultimate Reality (*Haqîqa*), which is the goal of one's search.

"The revealed law is like a candle lighting the way — as long as you don't hold the candle, you cannot travel. When you get on the road, your journey is the Path and when you have reached the goal, you have reached the Ultimate Reality (Truth). That is why it has been said: 'If the truths were manifest, the religious laws would be useless.' Thus, when copper becomes gold, or when it is gold already, it does not need alchemy (i.e., the Law). It does not need to be rubbed against the alchemical stone, which is the Path, for one should not ask for a guide if one has reached his goal, and it is a shame to send the guide back before reaching it. To recapitulate, the Law is like learning the theory of alchemy from a professor or a book, the Path is like using chemical products or rubbing the copper on the alchemical stone, and the Truth is like actually transmuting copper into gold. Those who know alchemy are happy with their knowledge, they say: 'We know the theory of that science.' Those who practice it are happy with their practice, they say: 'We accomplish these deeds.' Those who have experienced Truth enjoy this reality and they say: 'We have become gold and are delivered from the theory and practice of alchemy, we are the freed men of God . . .'"

Etymologically, the word *Sharî'a* comes from a root meaning "road." We have already seen that *tarîqa* means the "Path." It is, therefore, a symbolism based on the notion of passage, itinerary, pilgrimage. The one who takes up that road is called a pilgrim, *salik.* The *Sharî'a* represents the wider road, made for all men, while the *Tarîqa* is a narrow road, destined for the small number of those who want to accomplish *hic et nunc,* the realization of their full stature as Universal Man, or Perfect Man (*Al Insân-ul-kâmil*).

Given the diversity of character and the different spiritual capacities in men, the sufis say that there are as many individual paths as there are men seeking God. Every time one reads the Koran, one reads It as if It has been revealed at that moment.

Who are these sufis, who practice the *tasawwuf* and whose name is derived from wool, *sûf,* which they wear for humility? They always refused to give a rational explanation of the Path, as the knowledge (*ma'rifa*) they seek is at the opposite of science (*'ilm*) and is obtained only with the help of grace and spiritual teaching.

The Arabic and Persian treatises nevertheless try to give some definitions of the term. One of the oldest is found in Al-Hujwîrî's works. He tells us that the real meaning of the word "has been discussed at length and numerous books have been written on that subject. Some say that the sufi is called thus because of the wool mantle that he always wears (*jâma'i sûf*), others, because he stands on the first row (*saff-il-awwal*), still others say that the word comes from their claim to belong to *Ashâb-i Suffa* (Disciples of the Prophet), may God be pleased with them! Others declare that the etymology of the word is *safâ* (purity). All these explanations of the real meaning of sufism are far from satisfactory, although each is based on very subtle explanations . . ."

The treatise concludes: "Sufi is a name one gives and that has been given in earlier times to saints and spiritual disciples. One of the Masters has said: 'The one who is purified with love is pure and the one who is absorbed in the Beloved and has renounced everything else, is a *sufi.*'"

Here are a few definitions attributed to famous sufis. Dhu'l-Nûn, the Egyptian, said: "The sufi is the one whose language, when he speaks, reflects the reality of his being, that is, he does not say anything which does not exist, and when he is silent, his behavior expresses his state, and his state proclaims that he has severed all links to this world."

Abu'l-Hasan Nûrî said: "Sufism is to renounce all selfish pleasures." The renouncement is of two kinds, formal and essential. For example, if one renounces a pleasure and finds pleasure in that renouncement, this renouncement is formal, but if pleasure renounces him, then pleasure is annihilated and this is a case of real contemplation (*mushâhadat*). To renounce pleasure is a man's act, whereas the annihilation of pleasure is God's act.

Abu'l-Hasan Nûrî also said: "The sufi is the one who possesses nothing and is possessed by nothing." This designates the essence of annihilation (*fanâ*). The one whose qualities are annihilated does not possess and is not possessed, as the term "possession" can only be applied to things which exist.

Ibn al-Jallâ said: "Sufism is an essence without form," because form belongs to humanity, qualifying man's conduct (*muâmalât*), whereas essence is proper to God. As sufism consists in separating one's self from everything human, it is necessarily devoid of form.

Shiblî said: "The sufi is the one who sees in both worlds nothing but God."

'Al b. Bundâr as-Sayrafî of Nishâpûr said: "Sufism consists of a man's having no consideration for his external or internal self, but who looks at everything as belonging to God." Al-Hujwîrî adds: "I have related a few sayings of sheikhs on sufism so that the Path would appear to you clearly — may God give you felicity! — and allow you to say to the skeptics, 'How can you deny the truth of sufism?' If you would stop denying the names only, that would not matter, for the ideas have nothing in common with the things that have names, but when you deny the essential ideas, then you are denying the totality of the Prophet's sacred Law and its qualities. I beseech you in this book — may God grant you the felicity with which he blessed his saints! — to give these ideas due consideration and to meet their just demands so that you will abstain from vain pretention and acquire a perfect faith in the sufis themselves." (Al-Hujwîrî, *Kashf ul-Mahjûb,* p. 30 s., Eng. trans.)

THE BEGINNING OF THE PATH

The Beginning of the Path

To enter the Path demands a *metanoia,* a change in perception.

My goal is to know through the eye and the vision . . . the desire
of the vision tells me: Rise up and move . . .
In the same way that the child washes his tablet before inscribing
his letters on it,
God transforms the heart with blood and pitiful tears before
engraving His mysteries on it.

(Mathnawî, I, 1821 s.)

Come, acknowledge that your imagination, your thinking, your
sensorial perceptions and your understanding are like a reed
stick on which the children ride.

(Mathnawî, I, 3445 s.)

Therefore we have to look for what Rûmî calls *a second knowledge.*
The "conversion" of the mind implies that one goes beyond the plane of
common psychology and that "turning around" will lead to the understanding of the reverse side, the mystery of all things. The seeker must
"sell the intellect and buy the marvel of God." Thus, "the result of
religion is nothing but the rapture." (*Mathnawî,* I, 312)

Everything started with the cry of the craving soul:
Nourish me for I am hungry and hurry for time is a sword.

(Mathnawî, I, 132)

That search is, itself, an answer to God's call, for to look for the
Friend is to have found Him already.

Look for the answer in the same place that you found the
question.

(Mathnawî, III, 1120 s.)

"Nourish me for I am hungry . . ."
(Detail of a miniature of Bihzâd, 15th c.).

That hunger, that thirst, the *chawq* of the sufis, that burning desire, irrepressible, is the internal echo of the primordial Question which establishes forever the alliance between the Lord and the soul which has accepted its vassality. "Am I not your Lord?" and they answered: "Yes." (Koran, VII, 172) Likewise, the *samâ'*, dear to the sufis, is a means of awakening, of getting to the knowledge that illuminates, because it is the reminiscence of eternal musics. Again, this need to go beyond is an answer springing from the depths (*sirr*) of the being, for it is there that the treasure one is looking for lies.

The reality of knowledge consists, according to all the sufis, in admitting that man is unable to comprehend God in His Supreme Wisdom.

Abû-Bakr, the first caliph and the Prophet's dearest companion, declared: "Not to be able to comprehend understanding is already to understand!"

The soul which awakens to the truth at the call of the divine grace, which steps out of the sleep of forgetfulness, indifference and carelessness (*ghaflah*), is comparable to the mother taken by the pains of birthgiving:

The pain will be born from that look cast inside yourself,
and this pain will make you go beyond the veil.

(Mathnawî, II, 2517, s.)

From then on, it has to pursue its way, without respite.

By God, don't remain in any spiritual station you have gained,
but desire more,
The one who suffers from dropsy can never have enough water.
The Divine Court is the infinite plane: leave behind you the
place of honor. It is the path itself which is the place of
honor.

(Mathnawî, III, 1960, 1961)

When Plato talks about the "sciences that awaken the thought," he reminds us that the ascension toward the contemplation, the *théôria*, can only be done by stages or degrees. (*The Banquet*, 211, c) The symbol of the ladder that we find in Egypt's *Book of the Dead*, in the *Bible* and in the Christian mystics, is often used by the sufis in general and Rûmî in particular, for depicting the ascent. It works on two levels, cosmic and psychological. Commenting on the notion of *Mi'râj*, the Assumption of the Prophet, Rûmî explains that this ladder is the very being of man. "He ascends toward himself, from the exterior, which is darkness, to the interior, which is the universe of light, and from the interior to the Creator." (Sultân Walad, *Ma'arif*, Persian text, p. 121) The ultimate goal of the sufi's search is this spiritual experience, for which the "Nocturnal Journey" of the Prophet is the ultimate example.

"Crossing the skies, or the multiple layers of being which symbolize the concentric skies of traditional astronomy, he ascended to the Divine Presence."[7]

Likewise, the pilgrim on the Path, following this example, will try to clamber up the ladder of the universal hierarchy of Being. For Rûmî writes:

> At the moment you entered this world,
> A ladder was placed in front of you to allow you to escape.
> First you were a mineral, then you became a plant,
> Then you became an animal: how could you ignore it?
> Then you were made into a man gifted with knowledge, reason and faith;
> Observe this body, drawn from dust: what perfection it has acquired!
> When you have transcended the condition of manhood, no doubt you will become an angel.
> Then you will have done with this earth, your dwelling will be in heaven.
> Go beyond the angelic condition, dive into this ocean,
> So that the drop of water that is you can become a sea.
>
> (*Mystic Odes,* II)

The different stages through which the soul has to pass before returning to God are also described in the *Mathnawî*, as well as the state of unconsciousness which accompanies these variations.

> Man began during the reign of inorganic things. From there he passed into the reign of plants without remembering his former condition. When he passed into the animal state, he didn't remember being a plant either, he only retained an affection for that state, particularly in Spring when the flowers bloom. This affection is similar to that of a small child for his mother, he ignores the reason why he is attracted to the maternal bosom. It is also similar to the affection of the disciple for his spiritual master. The limited intelligence of the disciple derives from the Universal Intelligence. Then man entered the human state. He has no memory of his first souls and he will be changed again from his present soul.
>
> (*Mathnawî,* IV, 3637 s.)

We have to study this text in light of these two things. First, let us not fall into the trap of imagining travel as necessarily relating to space. Rûmî himself warns us:

> This is not comparable to the ascent of Man toward the moon,
> no, but to the ascent of the sugar cane to the sugar.
>
> It is not comparable to the ascent of a vapor to the sky,
> no, but to the ascent of an embryo to reason.
>
> (*Mathnawî,* IV, 553–554)

ومنه نوع اخر يشبه الذى قبله لكنه اصغر منه ولـه ثمرة ارجوانية اذا
اكلها انسان وصبى فى به بعض العوام منه و اصله مع الزوفا والفودنج
اذا شرب منه مثقال ا ن ح حتى الطبيع واشهاله

The cosmic "journey" of the soul is, in fact, a spiritual itinerary, like Dante's periplus through the different worlds. His description is similar to that of many sufis who were a great influence on him. Saná'i, the Persian poet whom Rûmî considers one of the greatest masters, has devoted a treatise to the nocturnal journey (*Mi'râj-nâmah*). Rûmî comments on one of his verses in the *Mathnawî* (*Mathnawî*, I, incipit and 2035 s.):

> It is in the realm of the soul that we find the heavens which govern the skies of the world.

And, as Rûmî himself writes:

> What does the heart that is intoxicated with the Beloved know about the road, the day's journey or the distance, short or long? *Long* and *short* are attributes of the body, the mental journey is of another kind. You have traveled from the seed to reason; it was not by making steps or by going from stage to stage or by going from one place to another. The mental journey is not affected by Time and Space, it is from the mind that our bodies have learned to travel.
>
> (*Mathnawî*, III, 1973, s.)

In turn, Muhammad Iqbal, poet and philosopher of the Indian subcontinent who died in 1938, commented:

"Reality is essentially spirit, but of course, there are degrees in the spirit . . . Through the whole scale of Being rises, little by little, the note of the I, until it attains perfection in man. That's why the Koran declares that the ultimate Ego is nearer to man than his jugular vein . . . The degree of reality varies with the degree of the feeling for the I . . . That is why man, in whom the I has attained its relative perfection, occupies an authentic place in the heart of the divine creative energy, and possesses, thus, a degree of reality greater than that of the things that surround him. Among all God's creations, he is the only one capable of participating consciously in the creative life of his Creator." (Muhammad Iqbal, *To Reconstruct the Religious Thought of Islam*, p. 80–81 and 120)

This analysis reveals two important points worth studying closely. First, the notion of "man capable of God" is a fundamental theme of Islamic thought. The notion of *fitra*, i.e., of the original nature of man, participating in the divine and created according to God's image, is essential. It is to restore this image that all his efforts should lead, and the "purifying path" has no other aim.

Besides, man has received from God, the mission to become the intermediary link between the Creator and his creation, the means for Him to manifest His Mercy and His Love, in becoming His co-operator and identifying with the creative power. Then he can say:

"Of his first souls he has no memory . . ."
(11th c. manuscript).   87

My image dwells in the heart of the King, the heart of the
King would be in pain without my image.
When the King commands me to fly in His Path, I take to the
skies reaching the zenith of the heart like His Rays.
I fly like a moon and a sun, I tear open the veils of heaven.
The light of intelligence comes from my thinking; the sky has
been created because of my original nature . . .
I hold the spiritual realm . . . I'm not the equal of the King . . .
But I receive from Him the light of His Theophany.(*Mathnawî*, II, 1157 s.)

This supreme mission conferred to man is a *mandate,* he is free to
accept it or not, but it is the reason for his eminent dignity.

Rûmî wrote: "Man is in this world to accomplish a mission. This
mission is his true goal, if he does not accomplish it, he has done
nothing. 'We had proposed that mandate (*amâna*) to the skies, to the
earth and to the mountains; they refused to take it up for they feared it.
Only man assumed it, but he is unfair and ignorant.' (Koran, XXXIII,
72) This mandate was proposed to the universe but it was unable to
accept it. Consider how many feats are done by the universe, they are so
great that reason is dismayed. It transforms the stones into rubies and
coral, the mountains into mines of gold and silver, it makes the plants
bud and gives them life . . . It is capable of all these mysteries, but is
unable to accomplish this one thing. Only man can do it. God has said:
'We have ennobled the descendants of Adam.' (Koran, XVII, 70) He did
not say: we have ennobled the sky or the earth. Man, therefore, accom-
plishes things that the sky, the earth and the mountains are unable to
do. When he does accomplish them, then he is free from ignorance and
perversity.

"God the Almighty has given you a true bargain. He has said: 'God
has bought, from the believers, their riches and their lives in exchange
for Paradise.' (Koran, IX, 3) The Almighty God has said: 'From you I
bought yourselves, your riches and your time. If you consecrate them to
me, your price will be Eternal Paradise. That is your worth in My
eyes.'" (*The Book of Inner Knowledge,* p. 40–41)

The ascent on the ladder of Being, prompted by the Divine Love,
makes the parts of the whole, dispersed in the multiplicity, reintegrate
into the One, like colours, when refracted through a prism, result in
whiteness. (See the apologue of the painters, p. 131.) The steps one has
to climb are numerous passages which allow one to escape what is perishable. Now everything is ephemeral except God's Face, says the
Koran. "His face is always present, actual, uninterrupted and eternal."
It is therefore the return to the center which makes the soul find the
heavens inside it. "The ultimate state for a man," said a famous sufi, "is
to go back to his first state." (Sarrâdj, *Kitab-al-Luma'*) Rûmî also speaks

of this *self* which, in the end, is conscious of escaping the world of illusion: "your first *self* goes back to your real *self*." (*Mathnawî*, VI, 3769)

A similar vision is expressed by Amiel, in terms that could be those of the Master of Konya. ". . . Disciple of life, chrysalis of angels, work toward your future opening, for the divine odyssey is but a series of metamorphoses more and more ethereal, where each form is the result of those preceding it and is the condition of those which follow. The divine life is a succession of deaths in which the spirit rejects its imperfections and its symbols and yields to the ineffable attraction of the center of the sun of intelligence and love." (in *Mysticism and Poetry,* by Eva de Vitray)

THE APPRENTICESHIP ON THE PATH

"When a novice comes to a sheikh because he wants to renounce the world, he is subjected to a spiritual discipline for three years. If he complies with what is demanded of him, all is well, otherwise he is told that he cannot be admitted to the *tarîqa*. The first year is devoted to the service of the people, the second to the service of God, the third to watching over his own heart. He cannot serve the people unless he is placed at the rank of a servant, i.e., he has to regard everyone, without exception, as masters, better than himself, and consider it his duty to serve them all in the same manner. He cannot serve God unless he has renounced every selfish concern, be it for this present life or for the future life. He must also show that he adores God for the love of God only, as anyone who adores God for a given reason adores himself and not God. He cannot watch over his own heart unless his thoughts are collected and he has dispensed with every concern in such a way that he stays in communion with God in his heart against the assaults of negligence. When the novice has acquired all these qualifications, he can wear the *muraqqa'at* (the patched garment the dervishes wear) as a true mystic and not as an imitator." (Al-Hujwîrî, *Kashf al-Mahjûb*)

The Experience of the Path

In the course of the itinerary leading to his spiritual realization, and in order for him to acquire the indispensable virtues necessary for attaining it, the disciple must submit to the discipline of the *tarîqa.* The cardinal virtues capable of achieving this "transmutation" constitute a way of living the truth, as the doctrine is a way of knowing it. In sufism, these are principally humility, charity and sincerity — the characteristics of the Prophet of Islam.

Humility derives from grasping the Divine Unity, as formulated in the *shahâda,* the Moslem profession of faith: "There is no God (or Truth or Reality) but God (Truth or Reality)." Only God *is,* everything else is subordinate to Him. As everything participates in the perfection, humility will consist in recognizing that any being in the universe can teach us what we ignore.

On the other hand, the whole Creation being one, man has to recognize "that by offering his soul to God, he is offering it to his fellow men. If humility is the death of something in the soul, or its contraction (*inqibâd*), the spiritual charity is an expansion (*inbisât*) which allows man to realize unity with all men."[8]

Finally, sincerity (*Ikhlâs*) or veracity (*sidq*) "is the apogee of the other two virtues and is based on them. That virtue, which generally characterizes Islam itself, signifies seeing things in their true nature, it does not veil the divine but reveals it." (*ibid.*) There is a *hadîth,* often cited, that tells us that the Prophet used to pray to God to grant him to see things "as they are." One of his companions, Abû 'Ubaidah, used to say: "I have never contemplated anything without God being nearer to me than this thing."

"The ascencion is the very being of man"
(detail of a 15th c. manuscript).   91

In the last analysis, as we are told by a great sufi, 'Abu Sa'îd ibn Abî-l-Khayr: "The Path is but one step. Taking one step out of one's self to get to God." In other words, one realizes that by leaving one's self (*fanâ*), nothing but God exists, or in another definition given by Djonayd: "Sufism is God making you die to yourself and resuscitating you in Him."

The spiritual virtues correspond to the "states" (*hâl,* plur. *ahwâl*) and their fleeting character makes them distinct from the "stations" (*maqâm,* plur. *maqâmât*) which are permanent "dwellings." "These states are gifts, whereas stations are acquired." (*Fal-'ahwâl mawâhib wal-maqâmât makâsib*), says one of the oldest treatises on sufism. All the texts provide details on the differences between the different stages of the Path, and chiefly on the gratuitous character of the *hâl,* which comes from the generosity of God, in the course of the war (*Djîhad*) against the *nafs* (or the carnal or lustful soul), which prevents the ascent on the scale, the *scala perfectionis,* leading to God. Here we should recall the triple division of man into body, soul and spirit. The spiritual itinerary exists essentially for the "pilgrim" to cease his identification with his psycho-physical being and to unite himself with the Spirit. The *maqâmât* represent the degrees one has to pass through in order to acquire a new level of being. Al-Hujwîrî says: "The station (*maqâm*) designates the fact of *standing* in the Path of God and accomplishing the obligations corresponding to that station . . . One is not allowed to leave that station before fulfilling these obligations. Thus, the first station is repentance (*tawbat*), then comes the conversion (*inâbat*), then the renouncement (*zuhd*) and then total reliance on God (*tawakkul*), etc. One cannot pretend to conversion without repentance, or to renouncement without conversion, or to reliance on God without renouncement.

"As for the state, the *hâl,* it is something which comes down into the heart of man without his being able to reject it when it comes or to attract it when it disappears." (*Kashf-al-Mahjûb,* p. 181)

These different modes of being, or different degrees of consciousness, that are the *maqâmât,* are linked to each other in a hierarchical order in such a way that, even when transcended, they remain with the seeker who has passed through them. The latter is totally transformed by each of them, he becomes this *maqâm.* About the *maqâm* of sincerity which, as we just said, constitutes the crowning of all virtues, the sufi Abû Sa'id al-Kharrâr wrote:

"In this manner, the seeker will see his states change and become easier for him. For each station that he endures for the love of God, hoping for his favor, he will obtain a reward of goodness. His character

The quest for the Simorgh (14th c. miniature).

will change, his intelligence will awaken and the light of Truth will fill him and become familiar to him. Evil and its obscurity will disappear and vanish from him." (Abû Sa'id, *Kitâb-al luma'*, ed. Nicholson, p. 42)

The stages on the Path are described very often and numbered. This is a classical example (See schema p. 95):

The number seven is constantly found in the writings of the sufis when they enumerate the "degrees" to be crossed on the Path. The great mystic 'Attar, who Rûmî said "had crossed the seven cities of Love," describes thus the road of the pilgrim. In a beautiful apologue, *Mantiq at-Tayr* (The Language of the Birds), he relates the quest of 30 birds (in Persian, *si morgh*) for the Divine, symbolized by a fabulous bird, Simorgh. Reaching their goal, they realize that the Supreme Being is nothing but themselves, the illusion of multiplicity having disappeared; the 30 birds *are* the Divine Bird. However, before reaching the end of their journey, they had to cross the seven valleys: Quest, Love, Mystical Perception, Detachment, Independence, Unity, Bewilderment and the Realization in the Annihilation (or Mystical Death, *Fanâ*).

This symbol can be compared to the one of the 70,000 veils which separate man from the Creator. A famous tradition of the Prophet tells us: "Allah has 700 (or 70 or 70,000) veils of light and darkness. If he was to take them away, the splendor of His Face would certainly consume the one who would see Him."

Al-Ghazâlî comments on this tradition when he classifies men according to the degree of transparence that the veil separating them from God has, or the degree of purity their idea of God has reached. (*Mishkât al-Anwar*)

In the same way, Rûmî has compared the different degrees of sainthood to the veil of light:

> The light of God has seven hundred veils: consider that the
> veils of light are as many degrees.
> Behind each of these veils stands a certain category of saints.
> Their veils diminish row by row.
> Those who are at the lowest rank, because of their weakness,
> cannot stand the light that faces them.
> The one who stands at the next higher rank, because of the
> weakness of his vision, could not stand a stronger light.
> The light which is life for the highest rank is only pain
> and trial for the one who has bad eyes.
> Little by little, the vision grows stronger and when a saint
> has gone beyond the seven hundred veils, he becomes the Ocean.
>
> (*Mathnawî*, II, 821, s.)

The Seven Degrees

The carnal soul	The admonishing soul	The inspired soul	The appeased soul	The satisfied soul	The accepted soul	The realised soul
The Journey *toward* God	The Journey *by* God	The Journey *on* God	The Journey *with* God	The Journey *within* God	The Journey *from* God	The Journey *in* God
The sensory world	The intermediary world	The world of spirits	The world of reality	The world of principles	The world of the invisible	The world of multiplicity and unity
State of the inclination toward the desires	State of Love	State of Passion	State of the Union	State of transition	State of wonder	State of the permanence in God
Dwelling: the breast	Dwelling: the heart	Dwelling: the spirit	Dwelling: the mystery (of the heart)	Dwelling: the mystery of the mystery	Dwelling: innermost depth	Dwelling: the founding of the mystery
Sharî'a	Tarîqa	Ma'arifa	Haqiqa	Wilâya	Dhât-as-Sharî'a (The Essence of the Revealed Law)	Dhât-al Kull The Universal Essence
Light: Blue	Light: Yellow	Light: Red	Light: White	Light: Green	Light: Black	Light: colourless

To be able to contemplate God without an intermediary, to witness His Presence (*shâhid*), one has to first become an ascetic, for it is the lack of detachment that obscures the vision (*Mathnawî*, VI, 2871). Talking about his father, who had become the light of God because he had gone beyond the feeling of personal identity so much that his "self" did not exist anymore, consumed as it was in this Light, Rûmî added: "This Light is not like the light of the sun and the moon, in the presence of which, things still exist. When His Light shines unveiled, there are no heavens, no earth, no sun, no moon. There is only this King." (*The Book of Inner Knowledge,* Chap. 3)

One of the oldest texts concerning the *maqâmât* in sufism, *Maqâmât-i-arba'în,* by the master Abû Sa'id Abî'l-Khayr, gives us precise details about each of them. Professor Nasr, who has translated it from Persian into English (*Sufi Essays,* Chap. 5), puts the emphasis on an important point; that the highest station described by Abû Sa'id is sufism itself (*tasawwuf*), for, to have become a sufi is, in fact, to have passed all stations and to have reached the Ultimate Station, Unity (*at-Tawhîd*), which is the goal and the end of the *Tarîqa.* The experience of these *states* and *stations* is a possibility given to any man who has pledged to lead a spiritual life with pure intention and who seeks them not as an end in themselves, but as degrees leading to the One. This One is higher than, and beyond, all states and stations of the soul and, at the same time, resides in the center of the human being, at the axe that unites all components, corporeal, psychic and spiritual, to their common Principal.

Now, in mystical theology, the three big divisions between the *Sharî'a* (the Law) (which, as we have seen, is formally prescribed), the *Tarîqa* (the Path) and the *Haqîqa* (the Supreme Reality), considered respectively as the root, the branch and the fruit of the spiritual itinerary, are represented in correspondence with four spheres of existence:

— '*Alam an-Nâsût*, "the world of humanity" which is perceived by the senses,

— '*Alam al-Malakût,* "the world of sovereignty" which is the invisible world, spiritual and angelic and is perceived by the intuition and the spiritual faculties,

— '*Alam al-Jabarût,* "the world of power" which is the celestial world, the world of the Divine Names and Attributes and is perceived in the union with the Divine,

— '*Alam al-Lâhût,* "the world of the Divine" which is not perceived because all phenomena are absorbed in Unity.

In their relation with the sufi Path, these spheres of being are described in this manner:

Miniature from the Topkapi Museum, Istanbul.

— *Nasût* is the ordinary human condition of the one who conforms to the *sharî'a,*

— *Malakût* is the nature of the angels that one tries to reach by following the path of purification (*tarîqa*),

— *Jabarût* is the nature of the power one tries to reach through illumination, *ma'rifa,* until one is lost in the next sphere,

— *Fanâ* is the absorbtion, the annihilation in God, in the state of Reality, *Haqîqa.*[9]

THE RECITAL OF GOD'S NAMES (DHIKR)

The brotherhood manuals, especially those of the 19th century, prescribe *dhikrs,* or invocations particular to each stage or degree of purification of the carnal soul (*nafs*). In fact, one can say that the *dhikr* is the principal method of sufism. It consists of praying ceaselessly, beyond *salat,* the compulsory ritual prayers. Rûmî said in the *Mathnawî* that the disciple on the *Path* must invoke God in the spiritual retreat (*khalwat*) until his whole being becomes prayer. The *dhikr* is the pivotal axe of mysticism.

The world, says the Koran, was created by God's Word (XXVI, 82 s.) and all revelation comes from His Word. Sufism asserts that the human word, in turn, can be used as a way back to God. "It is capable of expressing the Truth and transforming man . . . It has essentially two functions: to expose one of the aspects of the truth and to pray. The one aspect corresponds to the Divine Word which brings the Revelation and the other aspect, to its power of creating the world. In consequence, prayer is the substance of the world; to exist is to pray." (Nasr, *op. cit.,* p. 175)

To pray is, essentially, to remember God (*dhikr*). The Koran says to man: "Remember Me and I will remember you." (II, 152) A *hadîth qudsî* asserts: "Whoever will remember Me in his heart, I will remember him in My heart, and whoever will remember Me to an assembly, I will remember him to an assembly better than his own."

This prayer, taken "in its most universal meaning, i.e., in its unification with the rhythm of life" (Nasr, *ibid.*), will create a spiritual climate, a feeling for the Presence of He who said: "Where ever thou will turn, thou will see the Face of God living eternally." (Koran, II, 115) and that He is "nearer to man than his jugular vein." (L, 16). "Are not hearts in peace in the remembrance of God?" (XIII, 28). God asks that you should invoke Him and think of Him ceaselessly (the word *dhikr* contains this double meaning). "Remember your Lord in yourself, utter His name with humility and fear, in the morning and at night." (Koran, VII, 205)

In the practice of *tasawwuf, dhikr* more specifically designates the sessions of recollection. As prescribed by the sheikh and varying according to the disciple's station, it is sometimes solitary and sometimes collective. These sessions take place irregularly. The disciples (*murîds,* dervishes or *fuqarâs*) gather around the master (*sheikh, murshid* or *pîr*) or his delegate (*muqaddam*). Although the texts are different in each brotherhood, the ritual is similar. It consists of the recitation of Koranic prayers (notably the *Fâtiha* and certain verses) and sometimes mystical poems, and of chanting the beautiful Names of God and certain formulas such as this one: "I ask forgiveness of God, the Immense, apart from Whom there is no other god, He the Vigilant, the Living." Sometimes, seized by a mystic *hâl,* one starts to rock or dance (the organized dance, *samâ,* is performed only in some brotherhoods, like Rûmî's). Music also plays an active role, and we know, according to very recent studies, that the manipulation of tone and breath has a strong effect on the psyche.

Again, what really counts in the end, is the intention (*niyat*) and the total presence of the heart. Al-Ghazâlî said: "*Dhikr* is, in its reality, the progressive power of the Named, on the heart, while the *dhikr* itself wears away and disappears."

THAT THAT REMAINS

When a man becomes familiar with the *dhikr,* he separates himself from everything else. In death he is separated from everything which is not God. In the tomb, he has no wife, no riches, neither children nor friends. What remains with him is the *dhikr* alone. If he is familiar with the *dhikr,* he finds pleasure in it and he rejoices in the fact that the obstacles which were keeping him away from it have been removed. It is as if he was left alone with his Beloved. So man, after death, finds pleasure with this familiarity. Indeed, he is taken under God's protection and is elevated from the idea of the meeting to the meeting itself.

(Al-Ghazâlî, *Ihyâ,* III, 64)

Love

In the last analysis, everything is founded on love. God, as we are told by the Koran, is nearer to man than his jugular vein. The mystic discovers Him in his heart, if he loves. God declares through the Prophet's voice: "My earth and my heavens do not contain Me but I am contained in the heart of my faithful servant." And again, God said: "There is no other means for my servant to approach Me than to accomplish the duties I have prescribed for him; and my servant continues to approach Me by more unprescribed works until I love him. When I love him, I become the ear with which he hears, the eye with which he sees, the tongue with which he talks and the hand with which he seizes."

The mystic's love answers the given grace, the Divine's initiative. A traditional prayer, called David's prayer, is recited with these words: "Oh Lord, grant me to love Thee, grant me to love those who love Thee, allow me to accomplish the actions which will win me Thy love, allow that Thy love becomes dearer to me than myself, my family or my fortune."

"Love," said Djalâl-od-Dîn, "is that flame which, when it rises, burns everything, only God remains." The great mystic Persian poet, Farîd-od-Dîn'Attâr, affirms "that love's universe has only three roads: fire, tears and blood." Another sufi, Mîr Sayyîd Dhârif, said: "The cause of creation is Beauty, and the first creation is love."

For sufism, love is indeed, the soul of the universe. It is because of love that man tries to go back to the source of his being. Music and dance, the gyration of the stars and the movement of the atoms, the ascent of life on the scale of being, from stone to plant, from animal to man, to the angel and beyond; all this is due to love which is the astrolabe through which the mysteries are revealed.

"The fire of love is ignited by the melodies."
(dervishes in ecstasy, 15th c. miniature)

The soul, kept away from its ultimate reality, aspires to the meeting that will show it that the lover and the beloved are one. One of the parables of the *Mathnawî* relates: "One day, a man knocked at the door of his friend. 'Who is it?' asked the latter. 'It is me,' answered the man. 'Go away,' said the friend, 'I do not know you.' After a year of absence, burned with love and sorrow, the poor man came back. 'Who are you?' asked the friend again. This time the man answered: 'I am thee.' 'Come in,' said the friend, 'for you are me and there is not enough room in here for two people.'"

When individualization, which is limiting and is the cause of illusion, disappears, God is revealed as the only unifying reality, and therefore, as the only object of love.

> When a man and a woman become one, You are this One; when the
> identities are effaced, You are this Unity.
> You have fabricated this *I* and this *Us* so that you could play
> the game of adoration with Yourself.
> So that all the *I*s and the *You*s become a single soul and are
> submerged in the Beloved.
>
> (*Mathnawî*, I, 1785 s.)

The Koran says God has created all creatures for them to adore Him. He is both the adoring (*'âbid*) and the object of adoration (*ma'bûd*), and for Rûmî, this love is the meaning of everything that exists.

> The Beloved is everything, the lover is only a veil . . .
> Love desires that His word manifest itself.
>
> (*Mathnawî*, I, 30 s.)

> Love is an infinite ocean whose skies are a bubble of foam.
> Know that it is the waves of Love which make the wheel of the
> heavens turn; without Love the world would be inanimate.
> How is an inorganic thing transformed into a plant?
> How are the plants sacrificed to become gifted with spirit?
> How is the spirit sacrificed for the Breath, of which only a
> whiff was enough to impregnate Mary?
> Each atom is intoxicated with this Perfection and hastens
> toward it . . . Their haste says implicitly: "Glory be to God."
>
> (*Mathnawî*, V, 3843 s.)

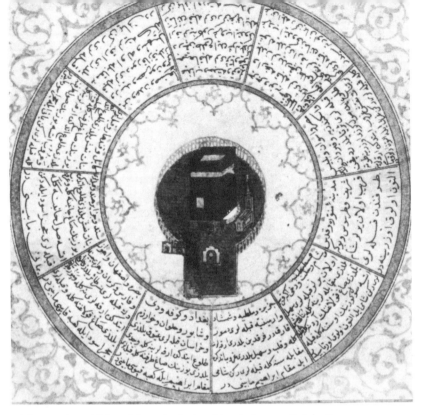

"Those who whirl and have in their midst their own Ka'aba."
(The Ka'aba, 16th c. miniature).

ON LOVE

"Where ever you are and in every circumstance, try always to be a lover and a passionate lover. Once you have possessed Love, you will remain a lover in the tomb, on the day of resurrection, in Paradise, and forever. When you have planted wheat, the wheat will surely grow, the wheat will be in the sheaves, and in the oven.

"Majnûn wanted to write a letter to Laylà. He took a quill and wrote:

Thy name is on my lips
Thy image is in my eyes
Thy memory is in my heart
To whom shall I write?

"You image lives in my eyes, your name is not out of my lips, your memory is in the depths of my soul, to whom shall I write, when you are wandering in all these places? The quill broke and the paper was torn away.

"There are many people whose hearts are filled with such thoughts, but they are unable to express them with words and form, even though they are trying intensely. We should not question this incapacity, for it does not prevent love, for love's sources are the heart, desire, devotion and affection. In the same way, a child loves milk and gathers strength from it but is nevertheless unable to explain it or to describe it precisely. He cannot express the pleasure he has in drinking it or how miserable and feeble he would be if he was deprived of it. It is simply that his soul is in love with the milk and desires it intensely. On the other hand, an adult can explain milk in a thousand ways, but does not enjoy it." (*The Book of Inner Knowledge*, Chap. 44)

> The drum of the realization of the promise is beating, we are sweeping the road to the sky.
> Your joy is here today, what remains for tomorrow?
> The armies of the day have chased the army of the night,
> Heaven and earth are filled with purity and light.
> Oh! joy for he who has escaped from this world of perfumes and colour!
> For beyond these colours and these perfumes, there are other colours in the heart and the soul.
> Oh! joy for this soul and this heart who have escaped the earth of water and clay,
> Although this water and this clay contain the hearth of the philosophical stone.
>
> (*Mystic Odes*, 473)

> At every instant and from every side, resounds the call of Love:
> We are going to the sky, who wants to come with us?
> We have gone to heaven, we have been the friends of the angels,
> And now we will all go back there, for there is our country.
> We are higher than heaven, more noble than the angels:
> Why not go beyond them? Our goal is the Supreme Majesty.
> What has the fine pearl to do with the world of dust?
> Why have you come down here? Take your baggage back. What is this place?
> Luck is with us, to us is the sacrifice! . . .
> Like the birds of the sea, men come from the ocean — the ocean of the soul.
> How could this bird, born from that sea, make his dwelling here?
> No, we are the pearls from the bosom of the sea, it is there that we dwell:
> Otherwise how could the wave succeed to the wave that comes from the sea of the soul?
> The wave named "Am I not your Lord" has come, it has broken the vessel of the body;
> And when the vessel is broken, the vision comes back, and the union with Him.
>
> (*Mystic Odes*, 463)

The story of Majnûn and Layla.

از گرم و افت تب

با غالیه با دو چون ستیزد

آمد بقدرکه زیباد

با آن بت مزکی چه خبر دا؟

از کش ملکش مخالفت

ای فرات چون کریزد

آید ز آنچه که درمنع

مریار زخود بدد کام

پی بر پی او شاد و بشا

با او دکان نهبه هسا

بهشت بریر نخل منظر

خرکا نشین بت بر پی وفا

درشگی آب ز د

چون لشکر نیک عهد

ایاج که دان از

چچون پریای پیدازا

آرام کرف و نفا

Love makes the sea boil like a cauldron; Love reduces the mountains
to sand.
Love cracks hundreds of fissures into the heavens; unconsciously,
Love makes the earth tremble.
. . . (God said:) "If it wasn't by pure love, how could I have
brought the heavens into existence?
I have elevated the sublime celestial sphere so that you could
understand the sublimity of Love."

(Mathnawî, V, 2735 s.)

Love has come and it is like blood in my veins and in my flesh.
It has annihilated me and filled me with the Beloved.
The Beloved has penetrated every cell of my body.
Of myself there remains only a name, everything else is Him.

There might be another face more beautiful than His.
And if there was one, it wouldn't matter, it is not my Beloved.
Renounce all the faces in your heart
So that the Face without a face comes to you.

If I look for my heart, I find it near you,
If I look for my soul, I find it in your hair.
When I'm thirsty and I drink water
In the water I see the image of your face.

You think that I am liberated from my longing for You,
That, without You, I have become patient and remain tranquil.
Oh Lord! Make me never approach joy
If I stay one moment without longing for You.

(Rubai'yât, "Quatrains")

Your soul is so close to mine
That what you dream, I know.

The friends know each other's innermost thoughts:
Could I be a faithful friend if I didn't know them?

The friend is like pure water to his friend;
In it I see my gains and my losses.

If for an hour you turned away from me
I would taste the most bitter gall in my mouth.

Like the dream which runs through the hearts,
Don't you see that I run through all these hearts?

I know everything you think of:
your heart is so close to mine!

I have symbols still closer;
Come closer and evoke my symbol.

Come as a derviche, in our midst,
Don't joke, don't say I am already here:

In the center of your house, I stand like a column
On the top of your roof, I incline my head like your gutter,

In the middle of your companions, I turn like a cup,
In the thickest of your battles, I strike like an arrow.

If I give my life for Thee, what luck!
For each life, a hundred universes!

In this house there are thousands of dead,
And you say: "Here is my domain."
A handful of dust says: "I was hair,"
Another handful says: "I was bones,"

A handful says: "I was old,"
Another handful says: "I was young,"
Another handful of dust will say: "Stop there,
I was someone, who was himself, the son of somebody."
You are in awe, and suddenly Love comes
That says: "Come nearer, it's Me, the Eternal Living."
(Diwân-e Shams-e Tabrîzî)

When this pearl was with me, I was filled with joy,
Shaken like the wave by the breath of my own being.
Bewildered like thunder, I told the secret of the Sea
And, similar to the thirsty cloud, I slept on the shore.

Since the moment I knew you through Love,
I played at the hidden game with you so much!
Come nearer, drunk, to the tent of my heart,
For it is for you that I have emptied this tent.

In the sea of fidelity, I dissolve like salt,
I have no more impiety nor faith, neither certitude nor doubt.
In my heart a star shines
And in that star are hidden the seven heavens.

He has come, he has come, the one who has never left.
This water has never been away from this river.
He is the treasure of musk, and we are his perfume:
Have you ever seen musk separated from its perfume?

Oh, my everloving heart! Toward the Beloved is a road coming
from the soul.
Oh, you who are lost! There is a path, secret but visible.
Are the six directions erased? Don't worry:
In the innermost of your being, there is a road to the Beloved.

Since Love has filled my heart,
My neighbor has not been able to sleep because of my sighs.
Now my complaints have diminished, my love has grown:
When fire is ignited by the wind, it creates no smoke.
(Rubai'yât, "Quatrains")

Man and the macrocosm.

The End of the Path

According to Sultân Walad, God's order to man to become His trustee on earth is one which man, created free, can accept or refuse at his own risk. "If man accepts this trust (*amâna*) he finds in himself, faith, and sees in himself, the Divine Throne and the heavens. What of the throne? He sees the Light of the Divine Majesty." (*Walad-Namâ*, p. 63)

Najm-ud-Dîn Kubrâ, the founder of the brotherhood to which Rûmî's father belonged, has commented on the Koranic verse stating the *amâna*: "In truth, I say, the *amâna* is what is described as the *great felicity* (Koran, IV, 17), that is to say, *al-fanâ fi'llâh* (the annihilation in God) and *al-baqâ bi'-llâh* (eternal living in God), and which designates the immediate reception of the divine grace; it is called the trust (*al-amâna*) because it is a divine attribute given exclusively to Man — i.e., to the Perfect Man who is the heart of the universe — and communicated by him to the whole creation. This is the mystery of the concession (*khilâfa*) granted to man alone. Man is *unfair* to the creation and to himself if he does not accept the trust, even though it implies the annihilation of his self. He is *ignorant* if he believes he is an animal who copulates, eats and drinks, and ignores that this animal form is but a shell whose nucleus is Love; for he is God's beloved and God's lover. (Koran, V, 59) Whoever loves anything else but God is ignorant of himself, and whoever knows himself, knows his Lord in a union (*tawhîd*) which transcends everything."

"The perfect man is the reunion of all worlds, divine and natural, universal and partial. He is the book in which are united all the books, divine and natural. Because of his spirit (*roûh*) and his intellect (*'aql*), he is a book of reason, called the Mother of the Book (*oumm al-kitâb*). This Koranic term designates the celestial prototype of the revealed books, the Word and the divine Spirit, which Jorjanî identifies with the primordial Intellect. In relation to his heart, he is the book of the preserved Tablet (on which are inscribed all things in the divine knowledge). In relation to his soul (*nafs*), he is the book of the written words and of the effaced words (the world of the transitory things one can sense). It is he who is these pages, venerable, elevated and pure, which should remain untouched and whose mysteries can only be understood by those who have been freed from the dark veils. The ratio of the primordial Intelligence (*al'aql-al-awwal*) to the Great World (*al'âlam al-kabîr*) and to its realities, is equivalent to the ratio of the human spirit to the body and its faculties. The universal soul (*an nafs al-koulliya*) is the heart of the Great World as the reasonable soul is the heart of man. It is for this reason that the world is called the Great Man."

(Silvestre de Sacy, *Notices et Extraits des manuscrits de la Bibliotheque royale,* 1818)

The perfect man, or universal man, "heart of the universe," is then a man who, having reached his full spiritual stature, is fully conscious of his essential unity with the One who has created him after His own image. He has been able to discover in himself that hidden treasure that one seeks elsewhere in vain, and which can only be found in the renouncement of the carnal existence (see *Mathnawî*, VI, 2540, s.). "The hidden treasure, hidden in the field of obscure representations, constitutes the deep abyss of human knowledge that we cannot reach." (Kant, *Vorlesungen über Psychologie*)

And Rûmî says:

Do not look (at the fakir who is looking for a treasure) as a
treasure-hunter: he is the treasure itself.
How could the lover be anyone but the beloved?

(*Mathnawî*, VI, 2259 s.)

Does not a *hadîth* of the Prophet declare that "the heart of the believer is the highest heaven"? Another *hadîth* says: "The heart of the believer is the Throne of God (*qalb-ul-mu'mini'arshu'llâh*)."

It is in his deepest interiority that man is going to find the universe again, for he is a *microcosm,* a reflection of the macrocosm. His spiritual evolution is therefore going to *correspond,* following the constant rule of analogy, with the evolution of Life itself on the Ladder of Being. This is the second meaning of the text by Rûmî that we have just cited.

Macrocosm

'âlam-i-hâhût The Divine Essence	latifa haqîqa The truth "The Muhammad of your being"
'âlam-i-lâhût The Divine Nature	latifa khafiya The inspiration "The Jesus of your being"
'âlam-i-jabarût The world beyond the forms	latifa rûhiyya The spirit "The David of your being"
'âlam-i-malakût The world of the imagination	Latifa sirriyya The supraconsciousness "The Moses of your being"
'âlam-i-ma'nâ The world of the spiritual perception	latifa qalbiyya The heart "The Abraham of your being"
'âlam-i-sûrat The world of forms	latifa nafsiyya The vital senses "The Noah of your being"
'âlam-i-tabî'at The world of nature, man	latifa qâlibyya The body "The Adam of your being"

The Arc of Ascent

The Arc of Descent

Microcosm

Djâmî, citing verses by 'Alî[10], shows that the doctrine of the microcosm and the macrocosm was known since the beginning of Islam. He also cites Rûmî in that context:

The Commander of the Believers said:
. . . You think you are only a small body, but in you the macrocosm is deployed,
and you are the manifest book (al-kitâb al-mubîn), through the letters of which, what is Hidden becomes manifest.
(As Rûmî also said): "As you are born from Adam, become like him and contemplate all the atoms of the universe in yourself.

What is in the pitcher that is not also in the river? What is
in the house that is not also in the town?
The world is like a pitcher and the heart is like the river, the
world is the house and the heart, the marvellous town."
There Rûmî — God sanctify his spirit — calls this world a *pitcher*
and a *house,* and the heart of the universal Man, a *river* and a *town.*
He indicates thus that everything that exists in the world is
within the human state . . .

(Djâmî, *Naqdal-nusûs fi sharh naqsh al-fusûs*)[11]

Man is the astrolabe of God who said: "Have we not ennobled
Adam's sons?" in the same way that the copper astrolabe is the mirror
of the spheres. When the Almighty God makes Himself known to man
and renders man conscious of Him, this man, in the astrolabe of his
being, sees, at every instant, every moment, the radiance of His Beauty
which has no equivalent and is never absent from the mirror." (*The
Book of Inner Knowledge*)

The place where God manifests Himself is, then, the heart of man.

The heart is nothing but the Sea of Light . . . the place of the
vision of God.

(*Mathnawî*, III, 2269)

But this is only true of the heart that has reached its full dimension.

It is not right to say of your own heart: "This also is a heart":
only the heart of the saint or prophet is higher than the
heavens.

(*Mathnawî*, III, 2248)

The individual hearts are like the bodies compared with the
heart of the Perfect Man who is its original source.

(*Mathnawî*, II, 839)

Because he actualizes the perfections which exist in ordinary men as
only potential, the Perfect Man, mirror of the Divine, where are reflected His Attributes, is the final cause of the universe:

That is why, in appearance, you are the microcosm, but in
reality you are the macrocosm.
From the point of view of appearance, the branch is the origin
of the fruit, but in reality, the branch has come into existence
because of the fruit. Had there been no desire or hope for the
fruit, would the gardener have planted the root of the tree?

(*Mathnawî*, IV, 521 s.)

Although God is absolutely self-sufficient, He uses the Perfect Man, His deputy on earth (Koran, II, 28), as an intermediary to make Himself known and manifest. Therefore, man is the *raison d'être* of the Cosmos and he is the link between the Divine and the creation. In his role as a mediator, he purifies as if he were a Sea of purity, whatever has been soiled. (*The Book of Inner Knowledge,* Chap. 8) He restores the union between those who have severed themselves from the Spirit and the Spirit. (*Mathnawî,* VI, 157) He is also the *Door;* the path to God passes through him:

> You are the Door to the city of Knowledge because you are the
> rays of the Sun of clemency.
> Be open, oh Door! For the one who is looking for the door . . .
> Be open until eternity, oh Door of Compassion . . .
> Everywhere is the place of the vision of God, but as long as it
> is not open, who can say: "Over there is a door"?
> Unless the Night-watchman opens the door, this idea does not
> cross his mind.
>
> (*Mathnawî,* I, 3763 s.)

> It is for me, said the spirit, that the King has liberated
> hundreds of thousands of prisoners (of this world) . . .
> Attach yourself to me, so you many know the beatitude and the
> royal falcons, although you are only owls.
>
> (*Mathnawî,* II, 1162–1165)

In the first parable of the *Mathnawî* (the parable of the king and the young woman, I, 36), Rûmî relates the story of a young woman who represents the carnal soul (*nafs*). She falls ill because she is separated from the King (the spirit of man, *rûh*), the object of her earthly passion. The King, who loves her, wishes to cure her. The intellect (*'aql*), who is the vizir of the spirit, intervenes under a doctor's appearance, but succeeds in only aggravating her case. So, the spirit implores God for His help. God sends him His Beauty (*Jamâl*), the reflection of the universal Reason (*'aql-il kull*) in the form of a saint, a Perfect Man and spiritual guide (*murshid-i kâmil*). After giving her the potion of the spiritual gnosis (*'irfân*), the Divine Doctor cures her and she is reunited with the King, the spirit, who was the real object of her love, for "love is the cure for all illnesses" (*Mathnawî,* I, 110)

The role of the Perfect Man as savior consists "in placing your image in front of yourself" (*Mathnawî,* IV, 2143), in revealing to the disciple, the divine who is within him. When the latter has arrived at his destination, he also will be a witness; his search will end with a return to his innermost self, his lost native land.

The
Maïeutic

The Teaching on the Path

Mawlânâ Djalâl-od-Dîn Rûmî intended not to elaborate on a meta-physical theory but to present a perspective and a means of salvation. His profound originality is not based on a new world-view, for his faith is Islam and his universe, Islamic mysticism. The true mark of his genius is to have had, to a degree rarely reached, the consciousness of the responsibility which befalls one who accepts the highest task, that of drawing souls from oblivion, and, in doing that, allowing them to attain their real dimension. He used to say:

"If we allow ourselves to rest, who will bring a cure to these unfortunate sleepers? I have taken charge of them all and have asked God to give them to me. If He so wishes, I can lead them to perfection, free them from the consequences of chastisement and help them climb the ascending degrees of heaven."

Profoundly marked by the directions he had received, first from his father, then from Burhân-od-Dîn, and by his bewildering meeting with Shams of Tabrîz, Rûmî insisted on the necessity of having a guide for the spiritual journey. "Choose a master," he said, "for without him this journey is full of tribulations, fears and dangers. With no escort, you would be lost on a road you would have already taken. Do not travel alone on the Path." (*Mathnawî*, I, 2943 s.)

In sufism, the bond between master and disciple is essential. By a contract between two free wills, a pact which goes back to the Prophet himself, is re-actualized. It is an initiatic chain (*silsila*), symbolic of the soul as vassal to its lord.

"Let the one who wants to sit with God, sit with the sufis." (*Mathnawî*, I, 1529 s.) The deep affinity which attracts one spirit to another, "which makes a bird fly toward its own kind" (*Mathnawî*, I, 639), pushes the seeker, who is himself sought by God, toward a master. The inclination of the disciple toward a master "is as natural as the inclination of a baby toward its mother." (*Mathnawî*, IV, 3642 s.)

Rûmî often stressed the importance of that propensity of the soul which seeks a total attachment. In one of his letters he tells this story:

"One day a man arrived by a tree. He saw leaves, branches and strange fruit. He asked everyone what this tree and this fruit were. No one understood his question, no gardener knew the name of the tree. The man said to himself: 'Although I do not know what tree this is, I know nevertheless that since my eyes have seen it, my heart and my soul have become fresh and young. Let's go and sit in its shade.'"

Because of such an experience, the actualization of the truths transcending symbols and images, thoughts and words becomes possible in the mind of the disciple; and the knowledge acquired in that manner brings with it its own certitude. Then, "this sign becomes a balm for your yearning soul, then you will say: 'Oh my friend, thou has said the truth . . . Go before me, be my guide, I will follow.'"

Only the one who has learned the realities through direct intuition, truly knows; (*Mathnawî*, II, 3566) "The souls dead in the bodies will rise from their shrouds" to that voice without words. (*Mathnawî*, I, 1931) And although it comes from one of His servants, it is always the voice of God (*Mathnawî*, I, 1936):

> If you were the intimate friend of my soul, for you my meaningful
> words would not be just a simple affirmation.
> If at midnight I say: "I am near you; come on, do not be
> frightened, for I am your parent."
> These two affirmations are for you, the reality, for you
> recognize the voice of your own parent . . .
> When you say to the thirsty man: "Hurry up! There is water in
> this cup, take it."
> Will the thirsty man answer: "This is a simple affirmation. Go
> away from me, oh you pretender! Go very far away!
> Or bring proof that this liquid is water coming from a spring."?
> Let us suppose that a mother tells the baby she feeds: "Come,
> I am your mother, listen my child!"
> Would the baby say: "Oh my mother, bring me proof, so that I can
> be comforted with your milk!"?
> When, in the heart of a community, there is a spiritual flavor
> (*dhawq*) coming from God, the face and the voice of the Prophet
> are like a miracle which constitutes a proof.
> When the Prophet calls from outside, inside, the heart of
> the community prostrates itself in adoration.
> For never in the world will the ear of the soul have heard
> such a cry from anyone.

The soul, this stranger, through the immediate perception of
this marvellous voice has heard from the mouth of God: "In truth,
I am very near you."

(Mathnawî, II, 3573 s.; see Koran, II, 182 "And when My servants
ask you about Me, in truth, I am near.")

The real master will then do everything in his power for these "sleep-
ing souls" to help them discover the Ultimate Reality (*Haqq*), which
they possess in the deepest of their hearts (*sirr*). In his carnal condition,
man is comparable to an embryo unable to conceive or imagine what
exists beyond his ephemeral envelope, and who, in the mother's womb,
waits for his delivery without seeing it. In an unpublished letter, Rûmî
writes:

> God has created the premises in such a way that to a drop of semen which
> possesses no hearing, no intelligence, no spirit, no seeing, no royal attribute,
> no slave attribute, which didn't know sorrow or joy, superiority or inferiority,
> he has given shelter in the womb. He then transformed the water into blood
> and the blood into flesh; and in the womb, where there are no hands or tools,
> he has created the windows of the mouth, the eyes and the ears. He has fabri-
> cated the tongue and the throat, and the treasure of the breast, wherein he
> has placed a heart which is at the same time a drop, a word, a pearl, an
> ocean, a slave and a king. What intelligence can comprehend He who has
> brought us from such a contemptible and ignorant state to our present level?
> God has said: "Have you seen, have you heard, from where I have brought
> you, and to where? Now again, I am telling you that I will not leave you here
> either, I will take you beyond this sky and this earth, to a very sweet land and
> a heaven that you cannot imagine: its nature is to open up the soul into joy.
> Inside that firmament, that which is young does not become old, that which
> is new does not become ancient, nothing degenerates or becomes corrupted,
> nothing dies, no awakened person falls asleep, for sleeping is made for resting
> and chasing away pain, and in that place there is neither sufferance nor
> sorrow." If you don't believe this, think for awhile: how could a drop of
> semen believe you if you told it that God has created a world outside its world
> of darkness, a world where there is a sky, a sun, moonlight, provinces,
> towns, villages and gardens; where there exist creatures like kings, rich men,
> people in good health, bad health, blind men? Now beware! oh drop of
> semen! When you go out of this dark dwelling, to which category will you
> belong? No imagination or intelligence could believe this tale: that there
> exists outside this darkness and this food of blood, another world and other
> nourishments. Although this drop ignored and denied such a possibility, it
> could not help arriving at it for it was forced outside . . .
> (One day) you will find yourself outside this world which is similar to the
> maternal womb: you will leave this earth to enter a vast expanse, knowing
> that the words "God's earth is vast" designate this ample region where the
> saints have arrived."

Only the soul born a second time can understand that "another universe" exists. The theme of the spiritual birth dominates all of Rûmî's work.

Sultân Walad writes: "A human being must be born twice; once from his mother and again from his own body and his own existence. The body is like an egg; the essence of man must become a bird in that egg, through the warmth of love, then he can escape from his body and fly in the eternal world of the soul, beyond space." (*Walad-Nâma,* p. 7, see *Mathnawî,* IV, 836)

Rûmî said: "The body, like a mother, bears the child of the spirit; death is the suffering and the anguish of birth." (*Mathnawî,* I, 3514)

In such a vision, death represents only a stage to be overcome in order to attain a new degree on the scale of Universal Existence.

Commenting on the Koranic verse, "You will surely go from stage to stage," Rûmî declared that pain, desire and passion are at the origin of every birth: "The body is similar to Mary, and each of us possesses a Jesus within it. As long as Mary has not felt the pains of birth, she has not crossed over to the tree of felicity. If we experience this pain in us, our own Jesus will come." (*The Book of Inner Knowledge*)

It is at the end of the preparation conducted by the master that the inner eye will open to the vision, the only real knowledge. It is toward this goal that all methods lead.

The Methods of Teaching

The sufi masters use many means in order to allow the disciple to "become what he is" and to help him "give birth" to the spirit hidden in his innermost self. He must discover that there is an abyss between what he thinks he is — what Rûmî called *a small man, a poor man* — and the sublime spirit which is his profound reality. The *spiritual harmony,* the person-to-person intimacy between master and disciple, the *symbolism* of the apologues which display the distance between the perceived sign and the signified reality, and the *dialectic* in which the student explores by himself, questions and answers and truths that he thought he had ignored, are some of these ways. The *samâ',* the spiritual oratorio, is performed differently by each brotherhood. The dance of the dervishes, as we have seen, is characteristic of the Mawlawîs. The *samâ'* is always a religious ceremony that creates, in the performer, a "state" in which he will be able to hear the echo of a call long sent, beyond time, and remember the world of eternal melodies.

The same principle is always applied: given that the disciples have different capacities, the master's role consists of adapting to their aptitudes. A famous saying of the Prophet declares: "Talk to men according to their understanding, and not yours, so that the words of God and His messengers will not be belied." Rûmî alluded frequently to that progressive form of teaching.

> When I am dealing with a child, I therefore have to use a language adapted to children,
> saying: "Go to school, and I will buy you a bird or I will bring you raisins, walnuts and pistachios."
> . . . Could the fire adapted to the working of iron and gold be good for quince and apples?
>
> (*Mathnawî*, IV, 2577 & II, 827 s.)

The master, by putting himself at the level of the disciple, helps him to *find again*, the knowledge. For Djalâl-od-Dîn, as for Plato, the *degrees* of the souls differ according to how much they remember, for they have existed before their terrestrial life. The spirituality of the sacred dance is attached to that reminiscence. A parable of *The Book of Inner Knowledge* illustrates the differences in this way:

"A group of people was brought from the country of the unbelievers to the country of the Moslems. Some were five years old, some ten, some fifteen. The ones who arrived at an early age, totally forgot their country of origin. After their education, all traces of it were lost in them. The ones who were a little older kept a few memories, and the ones who were older still, retained even more of the influence of their earlier lives. The same is true for the souls which have been in the presence of God. 'Am I not your Lord?' They answered: 'Yes.' They took strength and nourishment from the divine word, without letters or sounds. Transported into this world, in their childhood, they did not remember their previous state, and they felt foreign to the divine words when they heard them. This is the state of those who live engulfed and veiled by impiety and aberration. There are those who hardly remember that first Word, they have a desire and an élan for it; those are the believers. And there are those in whom springs the primordial state at the sound of the divine word, then the veils are drawn and they find themselves in union." (*The Book of Inner Knowledge*, Chap. 15)

It is because some souls have pre-existed together that some are linked with a mysterious spiritual affinity. The great Persian mystic, Abû Sa'id ibn Abî-l Khayr, said: "They recognize each other by their smell, like some horses."

"When your spirit fully recognizes my spirit, both spirits remember that they have been one in the past," said Mawlânâ.

The soul which glorifies God in this world, does so because it has done it during its pre-existence, and by doing so, makes others remember the day of the primordial alliance. "What is glorification?" asked Mawlânâ. "The sign of this day. If you have forgotten the glorification that your spirit should render to God, then listen to the example of the sages." (*Mathnawî*, II, 3137 s.)

"To be a master," said Kierkegaard, "is really to be a disciple. The teaching starts when you, the master . . . agree to submit to the examination, letting your interlocutor know that you are following his lesson."

The classic reference to this method is the dialogue of the *Méno:*

"The one who wants to sit with God, let him sit with the sufis . . ."
(detail of a 14th c. miniature)   123

Socrates: So then, does there exist, in the mind of the one who
doesn't know, true thoughts concerning these very things that he
doesn't know?
Meno: Of course!
Socrates: So now these thoughts rise in him like a dream.

(*Plato, Méno,* 85 c)

Likewise, in the *Mathnawî*, Moses, having asked God why He had destroyed the form after creating it, received this reply from God: "I know that your question does not come from ignorance . . . You are asking in order that the simple man might hear the answer, for you know the answer already; questioning is half-knowing." (*Mathnawî,* IV, 3001 s.)

Little by little, the Master feeds his disciple with the milk of knowledge, until the latter can dispense with his help. The "apparent master" then is only helping the "inner master":

There remains something else to say but it is the Spirit which
will tell you the tale, without me,
Or rather, it's you yourself, who will say it to your own ear;
Neither I nor anyone else, Oh you, who are myself.
Therefore, when you fall asleep you go from the presence of
yourself to the presence of yourself:
You hear what is coming from yourself and you think that it
has been told to you secretly in a dream.

(*Mathnawî,* III, 1298 s.)

What then can be *given* to the one who wants to be awakened? Ibn-ul'Arabî, the great Moslem mystic and contemporary of Rûmî, said that the mystic states cannot be explained but only *indicated* symbolically to those who have started to experience them. Rûmî compared that experience to footprints:

The presence of a friend of God is a book, and even more.
The book of the sufi is not written with ink and letters, it
is only a heart, white like the snow.
The provisions of the scientist consist of signs drawn by
a pen.
What are the provisions of the sufi? Footprints.
Like the hunter, the sufi chases game; he sees the tracks left
by the musk deer and follows them.
For awhile, it is the tracks which are his clues, but later
it is the musk itself which guides him.

(*Mathnawî,* II, 158 s.)

Be it through tracks, reminiscences, or recognizable signs, this procedure of the soul is always described in symbolic terms. In the end, it is always a re-creation of a lost unity.

The course of the seeker who answers the Almighty's call proceeds from the apparent to the real, from the visible to the unseen, from the sign to the signified. Therefore, the ambivalence of the symbol in the Scriptures will become apparent; it hides and reveals at the same time. Rûmî compares the Koran to a young bride who lets only the one who approaches her with love, see her. For the "words can only awaken an echo in you. They are the shadow of the reality, a pretext." They are useful only in as much as "they stimulate and make you seek. The word is like something you see moving in the distance; you run after it to see it . . . Man's word, in its hidden aspect, is an incentive to look for the meaning . . . a meaning you do not really see." (*The Book of Inner Knowledge*, p. 31, 86, 246)

The disciple must answer the kind grace of God with his own efforts, aided by the Master's help. "How can one reach the pearl by only looking at the sea? It takes a diver to find the pearl." (*The Book of Inner Knowledge*, p. 236)

The reading, the recitation and the meditation of the Koran gives the pious Moslem a constantly renewed source of spirituality. The incantation of the sacred text, the vehicle of the divine message, creates a magic to which is added the special resonance of the liturgical language, Arabic, which by its nature, can be interpreted on many levels. The level of comprehension is based on the spiritual capability of the reader who, reading the Koran as if It had just been revealed to him, is confronted with the symbols.

Looking for the hidden meaning with his own intuition, the disciple will understand that the parables are like a measure and the meaning like the grain it contains. "The intelligent man takes the grain of the meaning; he does not stop at the measure." (*Mathnawî*, II, 3622)

This point of view is constant in sufism. The great Al-Ghazâlî, whose work unites the strictest orthodoxy with the sufi mysticism, affirms that to interpret the Koran one must keep in mind the esoteric and the exoteric meaning at the same time. He declared, for instance, that there is no denying the fact that Moses had received the order to take off his sandals (Koran, XX, 12) upon entering the sacred valley where he saw the Burning Bush. "I say that Moses understood the command to take off his sandals as a renouncement of the two worlds, this one and Paradise. He obeyed outwardly to the commands by taking them off and inwardly by rejecting the two worlds." He added: "One should take the external as a symbol of the internal." (*Mishkat-al-Anwar*)

The passage from the visible to the invisible, from the appearance to the reality from which it proceeds, is illustrated by one of the stories which end the sixth and last book of the *Mathnawî*. It has a special interest for it presents many sufi themes in the form of a mystic journey. It is the symbolic tale of the wonderful citadel. (*Mathnawî*, VI, 3583 s.)[12]

THE THREE PRINCES

A King had three sons who left one day to visit the towns and walled cities of the kingdom. Their father had told them to go anywhere they wanted with the exception of a certain fortress decorated with paintings which, it was said, made one lose one's mind. That fortress was very remote and little known, and if the King had not forbidden his sons to go there, they never would have thought of it. But, their curiosity was awakened and they quickly proceeded to look for it. They arrived there at night. The citadel had ten doors. The paintings and the decorations filled them with awe. All of a sudden, they came upon a portrait of a young girl whose beauty dazzled them and inflamed their hearts with love. After much searching, they were told that it was the portrait of a young Chinese princess. Her father, the Emperor of China, kept her locked in a tower. They decided to go to China. They arrived at the capital and waited there a long time. Finally, the eldest prince, losing patience, went to the Emperor and, throwing himself at his feet, implored him to let him see the princess. The Emperor treated him very kindly and the prince fell more and more deeply in love. He soon died with consumption. Because the second prince was ill, the youngest brother attended the funeral alone. The Emperor showed the second prince the same kindness that he had shown the eldest, and over-whelmed him with gifts. Little by little, the prince became arrogant and ungrateful. The Emperor was indignant and inadvertently mortally wounded him. The third prince, who was the laziest, reached his goal although the story does not tell us how.

Djalâl-od-Dîn Rûmî has used this folkloric theme, well known in the Indo-European tradition. There is another version in the *Makâlât* of his master, Shams of Tabrîz. The commentary Mawlânâ gives reveals the importance of the tale.

First, he explains that the attraction of forbidden things is what incites one to the quest. The spiritual journey is an adventure. The ten doors to the citadel represent the five external senses and the five internal ones. The paintings are the forms and the colours of the world by which the soul can be distracted from its real goal. Nevertheless,

Page from the Koran. (12th c.).

بِسْمِ اللَّهِ الرَّحْمَنِ الرَّحِيمِ

قُلْ أَعُوذُ بِرَبِّ النَّاسِ مَلِكِ النَّاسِ إِلَهِ
النَّاسِ مِنْ شَرِّ الْوَسْوَاسِ الْخَنَّاسِ
الَّذِي يُوَسْوِسُ فِي صُدُورِ النَّاسِ
مِنَ الْجِنَّةِ وَالنَّاسِ

following the constant ambivalence of the symbols, it is the "adoration of the forms" that leads one to their pursuit. The awe which struck the princes is a very important step on the mystic Path. "The work of religion is nothing but wonder," states the *Mathnawî* elsewhere (I, 312).

The princes had started their quest without a guide, which is extremely dangerous. The first one died of love. The second, although initiated by the King, was lost by his self-conceit. The third prince alone had total victory over the appearances and the reality, although we are specifically told that he was the laziest of the three.

Another passage in the *Mathnawî* relates the story of an idle man who kept praying to God to provide for him and, to everyone's dismay, obtained satisfaction.

What Rûmî called idleness, one might better call passivity. There is something infinitely passive, totally abandoned in the heart of the mystic which calls for God's grace. It is a kind of virginity of the soul comparable to that of Mary in front of the Angel of Annunciation. Let us read the commentary of Ismael of Ankara:

"When God's Word enters someone's heart and when the divine inspiration fills his heart and soul, it is in its nature to produce in him a spiritual child having the spirit of Jesus who resuscitates the dead."

If the young idle prince is the only one to claim victory, it is because he did not count on his efforts alone. He waited with faith in the divine grace, knowing it would come to him. This passivity is a kind of silence, like Mary's vow of silence in the temple, as we are told in the Koran, which alone allowed her to conceive the divine Word.

The commentators differ in the interpretation of certain details of the story of the three princes. The Turkish commentary of Ismael of Ankara already cited explains that they go through different degrees of mystical experience. The differences in the various interpretations are not real differences but serve to illuminate different aspects. It is in the nature of the symbol to be read on many levels.

Despite the differences in interpretation, it is always the explanation of the journey of the soul when it comes down into the world of forms, and the adventures of the pilgrim on the Path which take him from the love of beauty to the quest of the Divine Beauty, which can be described only to the point of silence.

Recourse to the parables is frequent in the teachings of all the sufi masters. These tales transmit a moral, a mystic truth in an accessible and concrete form, which strikes the imagination and can be easily remembered. The details of the anecdote are often lost to the immediate memory, but when they surface, they emerge with their full significance and inner logic. The story holds all the possible meanings, which can be deployed when needed, for only the symbolic language allows the secret meaning to be revealed to each person according to his understanding. Such are the *Mathnawî's* anecdotes, often chosen from the folklore and actualizing the fundamental archetypes of these themes. They benefit from their more or less subconscious resonance which prolongs their echo. Following Sanâ'i and 'Attar, the work of Djalâl-od-Dîn Rûmî gives symbolism an essential place.

This work has been compared to Milton's *Paradise Lost* and Dante's *Divine Comedy*. It abounds with stories that are started, left and taken up again with no apparent link, but joined by virtue of the secret affinities of their spiritual significance. They use familiar images, often realistic and full of humor. Their number must not make us lose sight of their main purpose; this ample theodicy wants to be an initiation and an instrument of salvation.

"I have not sung the *Mathnawî*," wrote Djalâl-od-Dîn Rûmî, "for you to hold it or to repeat it, but to put it under your feet, so you could fly. The *Mathnawî* is the ladder of ascent toward the truth." Everything in it must be seen in that perspective. "If the mystics use comparisons and images, it is to help the man with a loving heart but a weak mind to understand reality." (*Mathnawî*, VI, 117 s.)

Therefore, everything becomes a sign. "We know," says Ibn-ul 'Arabî, the sufi master of the 13th century, "that God has described Himself as the Exterior (*al-Zâhir*) and the Interior (*al-Bâtin*) and he has manifested the world both as interior and exterior so that we can perceive God's internal aspect with our own interiority and the external aspect with our exteriority." "We show them the signs," says the Koran, "on the horizons and in themselves."

The sacred Book calls on that consciousness constantly: "To God are the East and the West, therefore wherever you turn you will see the Face of God for He is the Vast and the All-knowing . . . There is in the creation of the heavens and the earth, in the difference between night and day and the galleons which travel the seas loaded with good things for man, in the water God sends to earth to make it come alive after it has died, and in the fact that He fills it with animals, in the movement of the winds and the clouds that are at His service between the sky and the earth, in all these things are signs for whomever wants to understand." (Koran, II, 115, II, 164)

جزیره دارد سیاه و بر آن چشمه و حوش و دواب و جزیرهٔ دیگر برابر و

ان چشمها از آنجا روناس آرند و با فائق بر بذصورت بحرالخزر انست که کاشته آ

عرالخراسانی الخزری الدبوری بضی ازانت که باب الابواب بر انت و خلیج الخزرا

الدوایره خوانند و ان هزار و پانصد فرسنک ازجانبی بحرالخزر خوانند واز جانبی حریطه

ان و جرجان دو جسزیره بود و دران یکی بآب غرو شد و یکی را جزیره با کوه نان

The Purification of the Soul

The immanence of God to the world is only perceived by the purified eye. Mawlânâ says again: "When you are thirsty and drink from a cup, it is God you see inside the water. The one who is not in love with God sees only his own image in the water." Only the opened eye sees that "the universe is the book of the highest Truth." Only the heart polished by ascetic practices can become that spotless mirror which will reflect the Divine. A parable in the *Mathnawî* emphasizes this need for the purification of the soul.

THE STORY OF THE DISCUSSION BETWEEN THE BYZANTINES AND THE CHINESE IN THE ART OF PAINTING AND PORTRAITURE

The Chinese said: "We are the best artists." The Byzantines said:
"To us belong the power and the perfection."
"I will put you to trial," said the Sultân, "and I will see
which of you is right in your pretention."
The Chinese and the Byzantines started to discuss but the
Byzantines left the debate.
The Chinese then said: "Give us a room and give the Byzantines
one too."
There were two rooms whose doors faced each other, the Chinese
took one and the Byzantines the other.
The Chinese asked the King to give them a hundred colours; The
King opened his treasure in order that they might have what
they wanted.
Each morning, through his generosity, more colours were taken
from his treasures by the Chinese.
The Byzantines declared: "No tint or colour is necessary for our
work, we need only to take the rust off the walls."

"And in the mirror of the heart, the moon is reflected."
(manuscript of the 14th c. representing the Caspian Sea).

They closed the door and started to polish the walls which
became as clear and pure as the sky.
There is a distance between colourful and the absence of colour,
the colour is like the clouds, the absence of colour is like the moon.
Whatever light and splendor you see in the clouds, know that
they come from the stars, the moon and the sun.
When the Chinese finished their task, they started to beat their
drums with joy.
The King came in and saw the paintings. This vision, when he saw
it, ravished his mind.
Then he went to the Byzantines. They took away the curtain which
was separating the two rooms.
The reflection of the paintings of the Chinese struck the walls
which had been purified.
Everything the Sultân had seen (in the room of the Chinese) was
more splendid here. It ravished his entire being.
The Byzantines, oh my father, are the sufis, they are not
scholarly, they have no books and no erudition.
But they have polished their hearts and they have purified them
from desire, avidity, avarice and hatred.
The purity of the mirror is, without doubt, the heart which
receives innumerable images.
This Moses keeps inside him, the infinite form without form of
the reflected invisible in the middle of his heart.
And although this form is not contained in the sky or the
firmament, neither in the sphere of the stars nor on the globe that reposes
on the Pisces.
For all these things are limited and known — know that the mirror
of the heart has no limits.
Here the understanding becomes silent, otherwise it will lead
you into error for the heart is with God, or, more accurate still,
the heart is God.
The reflection of each image shines eternally from the heart
alone, in the multiplicity as much as outside it.
Those who have polished their hearts have escaped from the
perfumes and the colours, they contemplate Beauty ceaselessly.
They have abandoned the form and the shell of knowledge, they
have deployed the flag of certitude.
Since the forms of the eight paradises have shone, they have
found the tablets of their hearts to be receptive to them.
From the firmament, from the starred sphere, and from the void,
they receive one hundred impressions — what impressions? What
can I say? The vision of God Himself.

(*Mathnawî*, I, 3467 s.)

The first quality required of a mirror is its faithfulness. For the image
to be reflected exactly, its surface must be very clear. Ghazâlî said that
the divine reality can manifest itself in a clear and indubitable manner if
the mirror of the heart is cleansed of all the impurities of the world. The
neatness of the mirror is the symbol of moral integrity; the pure heart

reflects the mysteries. "My heart is clear like water," said Rûmî, "and in the mirror of the water, the moon is reflected."

The gradual corrupting effect of sin on the heart is compared to the slow accumulation of rust on metals. The ascetic practices are comparable to polishing, and sufism has always insisted on these mortifications.

Commenting on a saying of the Prophet Muhammad: "We have come back from a small battle to fight in a big battle (*Djihâd*)," Mawlânâ declared: "We have, up to now, given battle against enemies who had forms; we now have to combat the enemy of thoughts, in order for the good thoughts to destroy the bad ones and expel them from the body. The real war, the important battle, is this war, this combat." (*The Book of Inner Knowledge,* Chap. 13)

The lustful soul is essentially one with the devil, that is why hell is really within you. Its seven doors are pride, greed, lust, envy, anger, avarice and hatred.

The pure heart, purified from any terrestrial attachment, can remember God and invoke Him. The Koran says: "Is it not through remembering (*dhikr*) God that a heart can rest in peace?" (Koran, XIII, 28) The soul who remembers, wakens from forgetfulness. It is like the falcon who hears the King's tambourine calling him and telling him, "Come back." Another prophetic saying declares: "There is a means to polish everything and take away the rust; and what polishes the heart is the *dhikr.*"

It is only after these ascetic practices that the heart is capable of discrimination; for we can only perceive what we are capable of perceiving. According to a famous saying of Plotinus: "Never would an eye see the sun if it had not become similar to the sun, nor a soul see beauty without being beautiful itself." (*Aeneid,* I, VI, IX)

Thus, Harun, having heard about Majnûn's love for Laylà, wanted to see this famous beauty. Having seen her, he found nothing extraordinary in her. He summoned Majnûn and told him: "This Laylà, whose beauty has subjugated you in this manner, is not as beautiful as all that." Majnûn answered: "Laylà's beauty is perfect, your eye is mistaken. To recognize her beauty, one should have Majnûn's eyes." (*Mathnawî,* I, 407–408)

The purification of the mind must not be pursued on the ethical level alone, but on the mental one as well. Not only is purification morally correct, it also increases the power of the intellect. One must avoid all sensations which can disperse the intellect, and prevent real knowledge. Ordinary men, always attentive to the world's affairs, are in reality in a state of spiritual lethargy. Man is not only prisoner of his carnal nature, but also of his imagination and logical reasoning.

> Let us suppose you understand all the definitions of all substances
> and occurances. In what way would that be helpful to you? Know
> the true definition of yourself, that is indispensible. And
> when you know the definition of yourself, run away, far from
> this definition . . . a proof that has no result or spiritual
> consequence is vain . . .
>
> *(Mathnawî, V, 557 s.)*

For the spiritual world to be reflected in his mind as in a perfect mirror, the mystic, far from trying to decorate it, must constantly discard all the "illusory adjunctions." "All the arts and ornaments are like the jewels on the back of a mirror. The face of the mirror is stripped of these things." (*The Book of Inner Knowledge*)

The great Flemish mystic, Ruysbroeck, uses the same image: "Let your mind become a living mirror that is uncovered in front of God, for God to capture in it, His eternal reflection . . . Our thinking, pure of any image, is the living mirror wherein this light radiates."

To make one's self *transparent* to the absolute is, in fact, to become receptive in order to become illuminated. The instrument of this knowledge, which is drawn toward a suprarational mode to again find the unity of the spirit and the world, is not the reason — which is a screen — but the heart, in the Pascalian meaning of intuition. It is God,

Huwa (Him, a calligraphy in mirror form. (mausoleum of Mawlânâ, in Konya)

and God alone, Creator of the light, "who opens and seals the hearts of men," says the Koran. A tradition attributed to 'Alî, son-in-law of the Prophet says: "I know God through God, and what is not God through God's light."

Once free from everything which hides the spirit from itself, it is in its own depths that the spirit finds the Divine Essence, which is hidden because of its natural closeness. "It is because the Spirit is so near and so manifest that one loses sight of it," says the *Mathnawî*.

Another great sufi said: "The one who knows is not the one who borrows his knowledge from a book and then becomes ignorant when he forgets what he has learned. He is the one who receives his knowledge from his Lord, directly, whenever he wants, without study or teaching." ('Abû Yazid Bistâmî)

Once the heart has been cleansed from the exoteric modes of knowledge, one should not stop on the Path. "Do not stop at any spiritual station you have acquired, but wish for more," said Mawlânâ. He enumerated three stages on the path to knowledge: the opinion (the belief based on probability), the religious knowledge based on faith and the knowledge based on the mystical certitude.

"The intuition of certitude" ('ayn-ul yaqîn) is a *vision* because it is the only one which involves a subjective and absolute certitude. Talking about signs, literal or metaphorical, Rûmî remarks: "they receive many interpretations," but, he said: "the knowledge which is immediate and intuitive leaves no room for interpretation."

The mystical intuition, said Goethe, opens like a sudden vision. It is a flashing perception in which the notion of time is abolished. Such a direct apprehension is accompanied by a feeling of *presence;* for as the soul meets eternity in an instant, a transcendency erupts in it which it accepts and recognizes as such. This *presence* is defined as "a presence of the heart, a proof of the intuitive faith, in a way where what is invisible is as powerful as what one can see." (*Mathnawî*, I, 381)

More profound still, Mawlânâ defines this presence as *being present to one's self*. He conceives it, therefore, as the meeting, out of time, of the empirical consciousness with the inner and transconscious Self.

The Master wondered:

> Who is the one hearing my voice in my ear, who is the one who
> pronounces the words in my mouth? Who is the one in my eyes,
> borrowing my sight? Who is the soul whose clothing I am?
>
> (*Diwâne-e Shams-e Tabrîzî*)

Thus we see the sufis in general, and Djalâl-od-Dîn in particular, being well in advance and going beyond the present research in the psychology of the unconscious.

Another Dimension of Being

All of sufism is founded on the Koranic notion of mystery. From the start, the Koran emphasizes the necessity of believing in another dimension of things as a prerequisite to any knowledge. On the psychological level, it means believing in this fundamental intuition defined by Pascal, who said: "Man is infinitely greater than man," or Rimbaud, who said: "I, is another."

In the Western philosophies, from Plato to Heidegger, thought moves constantly in a field of permanent conflict; that of the duality of the body and the soul, object and subject. In contrast, the sufis want to establish an opening on a dimension which is beyond all duality, recovering the universal aspect of the inner consciousness.

The underlying unity of multiplicity is the essential theme of Islamic thinking, be it in the field of metaphysics, or in art and its symbolism. They both express this perception through arabesques, mosaics, theater of shadows, or musical or poetic impressionism, which all reflect the fleeting quality of things. "All is perishable," says the Koran, "except the Face of God." Any quest for the transcendental Self, which is beyond the spatial and temporal limitations, conveys the feeling of something missing, or a removal from the Being, of an exile. The sufis have sung over and over again of this nostalgia for the native spiritual state. Such are the sighs of the flute which accompany the liturgical dancing of the derviches. (see p. 46)

Eckhart, Plotinus and the Upanishads, as well as modern psychoanalysis, echo the same concept. "You are not only *yourself*, Oh my friend," it is said in the *Mathnawî* (III, 1300), "in Truth, you are the sky and the deep sea. This powerful You is a thousand times bigger than the ocean, in which a hundred yous could be drowned."

"We show them the signs on the horizons and in themselves."
(Koran XLI, 53). (Mystic landscape, 14th c. miniature).

The psychology of the subconscious leads, therefore, to a transcendental psychology. We are not interested here in the *subconscious,* but in a *supra-consciousness.* The Master used what we now think of as the customary premises of psycho-analysis, including the understanding of the psychological reactions created by the associations of ideas, as practiced by Jung and his school, the interpretations of dreams and the transmission of the *hâl* — spiritual state — from the master to the disciple (which does not exclude the transference that is dear to the psycho-analysts; rather, it is situated on another level).

On the other hand, the universal perception of the self leads to the discovery of the *inter-subjectivity.* Our fugacious personal states are linked through a common ego. This explains the parapsychological phenomena we can routinely observe in the sufi mystics.

Let us briefly go over some points we have just alluded to.

Psycho-analytical therapy.

In the first book of the *Mathnawî,* we read the story of a young neurotic girl cured by a divine doctor who discovers her secret illness by interrogating her. He uses key words and observes her reactions while taking her pulse. During the procedure, she is lying down, similar to a patient on a psycho-analyst's couch.

Interpretation of dreams.

We find numerous examples of this in the Mawlawî tradition. One outstanding example is the interpretation of a dream that the sultân of Konya, 'Ala-od-Dîn Kaykobad, had. Bahâ-od-Dîn Walad did the interpretation.

The sultân said: "I saw in my dream that my head was made of gold, my breast of silver, the rest of my body, from the navel down, was made of bronze, my thighs were made of lead and both my feet of pewter.

All the interpreters of dreams were unable to explain this one. Bahâ-od-Dîn Walad said: "As long as you will be in this world, your people will be as pure and as precious as gold. After you, in your son's reign, they will have the value of silver, after your son's son, they will have only the value of bronze and the creatures with lower thoughts will reign. When the power arrives at the third generation, the world will be in great disorder. There will be no sincerity, no faithfulness and no compassion among men of the fourth generation. By the fifth, the territories of Asia Minor will be totally ravaged and ruined; trouble makers will gain power. It will be the decline of the Seldjukide Dynasty; from everywhere people will rebel and the Mongol conquest will ruin the land . . ." The change of situation happened exactly as stated in the dream. (Aflâkî, *op. cit.,* I, 46)

ن ستوان نهاد که صبح اورا از سهو معصوم نتواند بود و من خویشتن را بهوده درو مال انگند من
عیش ایشان منغص نشاید کرد و آب روی و بیش مرد نشاید ریخت مهمان در زیر تخت می بود
نگوسار شد ذعیم اسف و علامت مصقول بر کشد . . . وز اسمان غمامۀ کافور بود مدد
کوی که دوست قطرۀ شعر کبود دریش . . . تا جایکه نان بعد از فرو درا
یکانده بارکت درود کرآب ستکی آهسته ازریخت بیرون آمد و بر بالای تخت بنشست ز
دار در خواب سلخت خوب بود نیک بازرمش پاذار مش برکرد و گفت آزاده تو احباب بودی من از آن رنج

دانیدمی و عبر ب دکر بیخحاطاز لکر می لیکن چون دوست تو درحق خود دانم و مشغفت تور
ذی شناسم و مقررست که زندگانۀ برای فراع مریح طلبی و بینایی برای دیدار من یخواهی اکر
بریشانی اندیشۀ از وجه سهو باشد نه رط و یعهد جانب دوست تو رعایت کردن و ازرم نهم
داشتن رهن لازم آید دل قوی دارس این نفرت خویشتن زا منت و همرا لیکن اکر لکر بابته نی
پیشه کرده بودم و انصبه یدیکاۀ داشته و زعهم هلی درمیان آله و ازجانین ختم زیا یشد
تناب آزل آله تاسهم همی ز درود ذکر و نفته نشوید و معان خردار روزه شعله و نور و تجمه

Metapsychic phenomena.

Aflâkî cites numerous cases in which the sufis were able to foresee the future or know about events happening at a great distance. Thus, Borhân-el-Haqq Tirmidhi went to Anatolia after a vision revealed to him that Mawlânâ's father had died. He then became Mawlânâ's spiritual master.

SEEING FROM A DISTANCE.

Shams-od-Dîn of Mardin consulted Mawlânâ about a difficult legal problem and Mawlânâ gave him an answer, a *fetwa,* that Shams did not accept. Mawlânâ sent him a more precise reply: "Shams-od-Dîn has, in his possession, a commentary on *fetwas* in two volumes that he bought in Aleppo for the sum of 40 dirhams. It has been a long time since he has read this book. Let him find it in his library and open it to the middle and read the eighth line; his problem will be solved." It proved to be true.

COMMUNICATION OF THOUGHT, TELEPATHY.

The sharing of a psychological state (*hâl*), between two people, produces a similar inner world. Communication between these two worlds takes place often through naturally occurring thought. Similarly, thoughts can read an event without the person knowing or any words occurring.

A child in the country told his mother: "In the dark night I see a dark shadow, black and horrifying, like a dream, and I get frightened." His mother said: "You should not be frightened. When you see this apparition, you should attack it bravely, and maybe you will realize that it is a product of your imagination." The child answered: "Oh mother, what if the mother of this shadow gave him that same advice, what will I do? And what if his mother advised him not to talk so that I am unable to unmask it? How will I recognize it?" His mother said: "In its presence, keep silent, and let him talk; wait for some words to fall from his lips. If this does not happen, then some words may come from you. If, in you and in your consciousness, a word or thought are formed, you will be able to know him through this thought, for being impressed by him, it will be his state of mind that will have passed through your mind." (Chap. X)

Transmission of a spiritual state (hâl).

The transmission of a message addressed to the innermost soul cannot be achieved with words, but only by the "silent word" that Plotinus talks about. Mawlânâ used the same term to designate this ineffable communication: *zaban-e-hâl,* the "mute word." Thus, in the *Kashf-al-Mahdjûb,* the oldest treatise on sufism, by al-Hujwîrî, it is said: "The language of the spiritual state is more eloquent than my language, and my silence is the interpreter of my question."

Any teaching presupposes this spiritual agreement which leads two people to the participation of an interiority, one that the Persian mystics call *ham-dam.* This beautiful expression literally means "being from the same breath." Thus, these words of Mawlânâ:

"I am not this body which is visible to the eyes of the mystic lovers; I am this taste, this pleasure, produced in the heart of the disciple when he hears my name. Oh Lord! When you receive this breath and contemplate this taste in your soul, consider it like an alm, and thank God, for I am this very thing." Between the master and his disciple, is established, within this agreement, a kind of spiritual osmosis:

"The good and the bad qualities pass from one heart to another in a mysterious fashion," says the *Mathnawî.*

In the person-to-person intimacy, the master knows his disciple's thinking. The *Mathnawî* ends with the evocation of this knowledge which can be obtained only through the mute exchange between two hearts. A child (i.e., the disciple) is asked how he will recognize someone in the night.

"How will you know his hidden nature?"
He answered: "I sit in front of him in silence
and make of patience, a ladder
to climb higher.
And if, in his presence, a discourse springs from my heart
which goes beyond the realm of joy and sorrow,
I know he has sent it to me from the depth of an illuminated soul.
The discourse of my heart comes from there, for there is a window
between the heart and the heart.

(*Mathnawî,* VI, 4912 s.)

Aflâkî reports the following anecdote: "When the sheikh Shihâb-od-Dîn Sohrawardî (the compassion of God be on him!) came from Baghdad, he wished to visit sayyed Burhân-ud-Dîn Tirmîdhî, the first master of Djalâl-od-Dîn. When he entered his home, the sayyed was sitting on the floor and did not move. The sheikh bowed and sat at a distance. No word was said. The sheikh got up after a while and left. The disciples cried: "No word was said between you! What does this mean?" The sheikh answered: "Between companions of ecstasy, what is used is the language expressing the spiritual situation, and not the language of words." (Aflâkî, *op. cit.,* p. 58)

The word alone, without the ecstasy, does not solve the problems of the heart.

"Man is a book," says Mawlânâ. "In him everything is written, but the darkness does not allow one to read this science inside himself." (*The Book of Inner Knowledge,* Chap. II) It will be the master's task to reveal his real inner dimension to him.

THE LEVELS OF COMPREHENSION:

DISAGREEMENT ABOUT THE DESCRIPTION AND FORM OF AN ELEPHANT

An elephant was in an obscure house; some Hindus had brought it to exhibit it.
Several people came in one by one to see it in the darkness.
Because none of them could see it with their eyes, everyone felt it with their hands.
One of them put his hand on its trunk and said: "This creature is like a water pipe."
The hand of another touched its ear, it seemed to him to be like a fan.
Another, having seized its leg, declared: "I find the form of this elephant to be like a pillar."
Another still, put his hand on its back and said: "In truth this elephant is like a throne."
So each time someone heard a description of the elephant, he understood it only according to his source. The various descriptions were extremely different! One man would call it *Dal* and another, *Aleph.*
If each one of them had held a candle, the differences would have disappeared from their descriptions.
The eye, our major sensory perceptor, is like the palm of the hand; the palm was not able to grasp the totality of the elephant.
The eye of the Sea is one thing, the foam, another. Leave the foam there and look with the eye of the Sea.
The spray which comes off the waves moves night and day; you see the foam, not the sea. How strange!
We knock against each other like little boats;
Our eyes are blinded although we are in clear water.
Oh you, who have fallen asleep in the boat of the body, you have seen the water, now contemplate the Water of the water.
The water has a Water that directs it, the spirit has a Spirit that calls it.

(Mathnawî, III, 1270 s.)

A Bihzâd miniature, 15th c.

THE HIDDEN TREASURE

A citizen of Baghdad had wasted all of his inheritance and he was poverty-stricken. After he had addressed fervent prayers to God, he dreamt and heard a voice telling him that there was, in Cairo, a treasure hidden at a certain place. Having arrived in Cairo without any money, he decided to beg but he was ashamed to do it before nightfall. As he was meandering the streets, a police patrol seized him, mistaking him for a thief, and beat him up before he could explain. In the end he was able to talk and told his dream with such sincerity in his voice that the Chief of Police was convinced by it. The latter said: "I see that you are not a thief, you are a good man, but how have you been stupid enough to make such a long journey on the basis of a dream? I myself have often dreamt of a treasure hidden in Baghdad (and he named a street and house number) and I have never undertaken the journey." In fact, the house he mentioned was the house of our hero. The latter, giving thanks to God for his good fortune and realizing that the cause of his misfortune was his own error, returned to Baghdad, where he found the treasure hidden in his own house.

(*Mathnawî*, VI, 4206 s.)

Thus, it is inside ourselves that we should be looking for the real treasure; however, this discovery can be made only after *one leaves home* and with the intercession of a *foreigner*. The role of the master consists of turning the disciple's mind toward his own center. As we read in the work of another Persian sufi, Abû Sa'id ibn Abî-l-Khayr, "The Path is only one step; make one step out of yourself to get to God. Leaving one's self is to realize that this self does not exist, and that nothing exists except God."

THE REAL KNOWLEDGE

A King had confided his son to the masters of knowledge so that they could instruct him in the sciences of Astronomy, the Occult and other subjects. The son had succeeded in his studies, in spite of his lack of intelligence. One day the King took a ring in his hand and, as he wanted to test his son, asked him to tell him what he held. The son replied: "What you have in your hand is something round, yellow and hollow." The King said: "These indications are right, but what is it in reality?" The prince answered: "It must be a sieve." The King said: "Now, now, you have just given such precise indications that the mind is awed by the power of your knowledge, but how can you not understand that a sieve is too large to be contained in my hand?" In the same way, the scientists of today are very meticulous in their research; they understand completely, that which is of no concern to them, and they want to understand everything in this way. As to their own person, they ignore it just as completely. Morally, they know what can and cannot be done, saying: "This is allowed and that is not allowed. That is lawful and this is unlawful." However, they can't make the same distinctions when it concerns their own beings.

That an object is round, yellow and hollow, is only an accident. If you throw it in the fire, none of these attributes will remain; it will become a pure essence. It's the same with the appearances of sciences, actions or words. Appearances do not depend on the essence of the thing considered, yet only the essence survives. Thus, the scientists who talk of all these things, explaining them and judging them, are like the boy thinking that his father held a sieve. They are ignorant of the principles governing the things they are talking about.

(*The Book of Inner Knowledge*, Chap. 4)

YOU WOULD NOT BE LOOKING FOR ME IF YOU HAD NOT FOUND ME ALREADY

As long as you do not look for something, you do not find it. However, the Beloved is an exception — before you find him you do not look for him.
Man desires something that he has not found, he looks for it day and night, but it would be amazing if his search continued after he had found the object of his desire. A desire fixed on an object already found is not of the human spirit. Man cannot imagine such a desire because he is always attracted by novelty. The search which concerns something already found is proper to God, for God Almighty has everything in His power. *The one who finds is the Magnanimous,* for the One who finds is the One who has found everything. *Kun fa yakûn (Be, and it is).* The Almighty God is the Seeker for *"it is He who is the Seeker and the Dominator."* That is the meaning of this saying: "Oh man, as long as you remain in this ephemeral search, you are far from the goal. When your search is annihilated in the search for God and when the search coming from God is greater than yours, then you become a real seeker because of the search of God."

(*The Book of Inner Knowledge*, Chap. 51)

The Presence
of Sufism

A saying of the Prophet (*hadîth*) declares that "God is beautiful and loves what is beautiful." Ibn ul'Arabî commented on it, saying: "If God loves the beauty of forms, it is because they reflect His beauty in the same way that they reflect the Being."

Another famous *hadîth* says that the "spiritual virtue" (*ihsân*), which is the very essence of sufism, is to adore God, as if we were seeing Him; for if we do not see Him, He sees us. The term *ihsân* comes from a root meaning beauty. Therefore, we should be contemplating the universe in the light of this spirituality, and it is within the *Path* that reside all the principles governing an Islamic work of art. This art is nothing but the reflection of the spirit, and even of the form of the Koranic Revelation, in the world of matter. All the elements which compose a work of art — space, form, light and colour — have to be studied from that point of view. (Nasr, *The Sense of Unity,* introduction)

Beauty is sacred and its contemplation makes one participate in the holiness.

What God said to the rose, that made its beauty bloom,
He has said to my heart and made it 100 times more beautiful.
(*Mathnawî,* III, 4129)

Each creature is, in reality, a witness (*shâhid*) of the Divine Beauty.

Know, oh my son, that each thing in the universe is a vessel full to the brim with wisdom and beauty. It is also a drop from the river of His beauty . . . It is a hidden treasure because of its plentitude, it has exploded and made the earth more brilliant than the skies. It is a hidden treasure because of its plentitude, it has sprung up and made the earth like a sultân wearing a satin robe.
(*Mathnawî,* I, 2860 s.)

Rûmî insisted on the numinous effect of beauty, which throws the viewer into bewilderment and wonder.

I remain in astonishment, venerating this beauty; "God is great," is, at every moment, on the lips of my heart.

Mystic Odes, 499)

The power that art has for creating the sacred consists of *taking back*. The sufi term *tâ'wil,* indicates this procedure of going from the multiplicity of forms to the underlying Unity, according to the vision of Islam. Thus, the creative man *repeats* the creation with the help of *rites*. The *Sharî'a,* the religious law, impregnates the whole of one's existence with its rhythms which are linked to the cosmos. Every prayer means being in unison with a sacred universe, in which the bird prays when he deploys his wings, and the tree, when it makes a shadow, as we read in the Koran.

The awakened soul which tries to manifest itself in a work of art, will use natural sciences, numbers, lines and colours. The internal beauty of matter has been liberated for the artist in proportion to the degree of comprehension he has attained. It is by integrating the internal and external aspects of his being, through whatever medium he has chosen, that the artist arrives at spiritual perfection. "Spiritual virtue," as we have seen, is, in itself, beauty.

The fundamental postulate here is the existence, in everything and everywhere, of an internal aspect, (*bâtin*), *qualitative,* a hidden meaning; and an external one, visible (*zâhir*), *quantitative.*

With a perspective such as this one, the symbolism of the center can be applied to all levels. We learned that in the transcendental psychology of sufism, the problem is always one of going from the sign to the signified; or, in other words, from the darkness which is the exterior to the light which is interior, as Rûmî said. For instance, the architect uses, as a reference, a cosmic model; the building will be constructed around a hearth, the house will have a patio, the garden a fountain in its middle, reflecting the trees. The mosque will be oriented toward the Center of centers, the Ka'aba in Mecca — itself, a symbol of the Spirit.

In the *Sense of Unity,* a treatise on the sufi tradition in Persian architecture, the authors remark that space is the place of the "hidden treasure." The house is compared to the body of man; the body encloses the soul, which contains the spirit. The walls are conceived as the means to isolate and to define a sacred place. We know that it is the same for a prayer rug which is, literally, a temple.

As for man, a microcosm reflecting a macrocosm, he contains in himself all the potentials of the universe in his seven subtle (*latif*) centers.

According to Rûmî, he is an isthmus between two darknesses; he is situated between the sensitive and the intelligible worlds, and in his own being, between a subconscious and supraconscious.

The qualities of man are the theophanies of the seven personal qualities of the Divinity: Life, Knowledge, Will, Power, Hearing, Seeing and the Word. (See the schema, p. 95) The archetype of the Creation is the Perfect Man, the end of the Path, the final cause and *goal of the universe*. As Rûmî said, he has become the mirror of the Divine Attributes, which he actualizes and totalizes; just as the content of a work of art (*bâtin*) is a "symbolic recapitulation of its archetype." (*op. cit.*)

We find the exact homologue for the master-disciple relationship in the crafts corporations, which also revolved around a spiritual master of the given craft.

SUFISM AND CULTURE

Many sufis were not only ascetic men, but poets exalting the divine love. It is impossible to name them all.[13] Let us recall a few: Basra's woman saint, Râbi'a 'Adawîyya, Dhû'n-Nûn al-Misrî, al-Hallâdj, that the works of L. Massignon has made famous in the West, all of whom lived during the first centuries of Islam. Omar ibn al-Fâridh was a contemporary of Rûmî and Sanâ'î. 'Attar preceded him and Djâmî and Mahmud Shabestârî came a little later (14th and 15th centuries). Most of them were mystics and theoreticians, including Mohâsibî (d. 857) and 'Abd Allah al-Ansârî (d. 1088). Sanâ'î wrote the *Hadiqat,* 'Attar, the *Memorial of Saints,* Djâmî, the *Nafahât-al-Uns,* Shabestârî, the admirable *Golshan-i-Raz* (*The Rosegarden of Mysteries*) and Rûmî, many works of which the *Mathnawî* is perhaps the most important. All of these are great works of mystic thought. The greatest of the mystic poets was Ibn-ul'Arabî, (1165–1240), author of hundreds of works. The principal ones are *Fusus-al-Hikam* (*The Wisdom of the Prophets*) and *Futûhat al Makkiya* (*The Meccan Revelations*). Some wrote in Arabic, some in Persian and others in Turkish like the great poet Yunus Emre (14th century). All of these we have named, even those who were of Iranian origin, were sunnis, not shi'ites, as is the case with the great majority of sufis.

As for the treatises of sufism in prose, the oldest we know of are Harawî's and al-Hujwîrî's in Persian, and Sarrâdj's and Qushayrî's in Arabic. These all date from the 11th century.

Sufism has also inspired a whole tradition of poetry and music in circles much simpler than the very cultured ones, and in the vernacular.

The brotherhoods were a bridge between the intellectuality of the high mystic spheres and popular devotion. It is the sufi poets who wrote songs of devotion and prayer in the various dialects of the masses, which became vehicles of culture to these people.

Ironically, this popular devotion played a part in the decline of sufism. The Islamic orthodoxy has often taken a position against maraboutism — cults of local saints which engender legends, frenetic manifestations, trances, etc. These are superstitions and deviations and have nothing to do with Islam as such, and exist in all religions.

On a more doctrinal level, the attacks of the doctors of the Law (*'ulamâ*) were persistent, if intermittent, during the history of sufism. These doctors considered mysticism as unorthodox. The great philosopher, Al-Ghazâlî (d. 1111), whose authority is uncontested, succeeded in allying the purest orthodoxy with sufism. His personal experience allowed him to understand that there was no incompatibility between the two. Closer to us in time, the poet and thinker, Mohammad Iqbal (d. 1938), in the course of the remarkable conferences, *To Reconstruct the Religious Thought of Islam,* has shown with finesse, the differences between a false and overly-passive mysticism and the real sufism, which is the true inner dimension of Islam.

It is impossible to give precise information about the present situation of the brotherhoods in the Islamic world. Some are disappearing, others have been abolished by governmental decisions, while still others survive in a more or less clandestine fashion. In spite of it all, according to the author of an important book on the sufi orders, "The true sufi tradition of initiation and spiritual direction continues and will never be lost. The Path, in our epoch as in the old days, is for the small number of men who are ready to pay the necessary price. The vision of these few men who, while following the road of a personal meeting, escape the Times, and are able to know the re-creation, is still vital to the spiritual good of humanity." (J. Spencer-Trimingham, *op. cit.*)

As Rûmî said:

When the soul has been fertilized by the Soul of the soul,
by such a soul, the world has been fertilized.

(*Mathnawî*, II, 1184 s.)

The brotherhoods have played an immense role in the traditional societies of the Islamic world. People were born and lived their lives in the shadow of the *zâouia,* where members of the orders met and to which most were attached by familial links. The Koran was recited there, and people grew up listening to their songs, watching their dances, in the atmosphere of the protection and intercession of their saints. The *zâouia* was a privileged place for prayer and meditation, and a living presence of the faith. The humblest mausoleum was a recollection of spiritual realities. The brotherhoods have also always had an educational function, taking charge of the religious teaching, and a mission of consolation to the poorer classes, especially during difficult times. These aspects of the brotherhoods are in keeping with their status as a popular religion. There is no class distinction for the sufis; the members are a real family and they extend this sentiment to all other people. There was a place for women in the sufi orders and some organized circles for women alone. In Konya, Rûmî used to go and visit them regularly, and directed their prayer meetings.

The brotherhoods (Bektashîyya and Khalwatîyya) could be urban or rural. Some were more purely regional, such as the Bektashîyya in Turkey, the Badawîyya in Egypt and the Chishtîyya in India. Others, like the Qâdirîyya, exist in most countries. The Mawlawîyya, as we have said, can be found in the whole Islamic world.

The differences in cultures have influenced the brotherhoods and some religious practices vary according to the location of the *tarîqa,* be it in Indonesia, the Maghreb, or Black Africa, without changes in the fundamental principles.

HISTORY OF THE BROTHERHOODS

Though sufism may go back to the very first centuries of Islam, because it represents, on a doctrinal plane, "the underlying mystery of the Koran" and the spirit of the religion as the practical side of the Path, it was institutionalized much later. The first masters of the *tasawwuf* would gather around them, those disciples seeking a spiritual direction. Many of these would spend a large part of their lives on the road, seeking more learning. Soon, centers were built, called *ribât, Khânaqa* or *zâouia,* where they would spend some time on their way. They could be found in Damascus, Palestine, Khorassan and Alexandria as early as the 8th century A.D. (200 heggire). They were sponsored by pious dona-

A zâouia in Miliana.

tions (*awkaf*). During the 11th century, they became the seats of *tarîqas*, mystical schools claiming a founding member and teaching certain rules of life and spiritual exercises coming from a long continuous "chain" (*silsila*) going back to the Prophet himself.

These *tarîqas* began to require the special relationship between master (*murshid*) and disciple. The master not only gave his teachings but also spiritual guidance on the Path fixed by a tradition inherited from the founder, one that he would have to transmit in his turn. All were firmly established within the Islamic orthodoxy and did not reject any of its obligations.

The names of the greatest sufi masters were included in the *isnads* (mystical genealogies) of the *tarîqas*. The most famous are Abu'l Qâsim al Djonayd (d. 910) and Bayazîd al-Bistâmî (d. 874). They embody the two different tendencies of sufism; Bistâmî's was characterized by ecstasy (*ghalaba*) and the mystical exaltation (*sukr*), Djonayd's by sobriety (*sahw*). "It is the most famous of all doctrines, all the sheikhs have adopted it." (Kashf al-Mahjûb, translated by R. A. Nicholson, London, 1936, p. 184–185) Approved by the orthodoxy, Djonayd came to be considered as *The Sheikh of the Path,* the common ancestor of most brotherhoods.

Naqshabandîya brotherhood in Afghanistan.

The most important *tarîqas* among the institutionalized sufi orders are the following:

The Sohrawardîya. The history of this brotherhood begins with Diyâ-od-Dîn Sohrawardî (d. 1168) because of the influence he exercised on his nephew, Shihâb-od-Dîn, who is considered the real founder. Diyâ-od-Dîn associated in his youth with the great sheikh, Ahmad al-Ghazâlî, and lived in seclusion. He had numerous disciples. Among them, Rûzbehân Baqlî of Shîraz, Ismâ'îl al-Qaarî and 'Ammar al-Bidlîsî. These last two were the masters of the great mystic, Namj-od-Dîn, founder of the Kubrâwiyya, one of the oldest brotherhoods.

Shihâb od-Dîn (1145–1234) received his first teachings from his uncle. The caliph, an-Nâsir, held him in great esteem and sent him as an ambassador to 'Ala-od-Dîn Kaykobâd, the Seldjukide sultân of Konya during Rûmî's life.

Djâmî relates that when Bahâ-od-Dîn Walad arrived in Baghdad, he was asked where he came from and where he was going. He answered: "From God to God, there is nothing but God." These words were repeated to Shihâb od-Dîn Sohrawardî, who said: "That can only be Bahâ-od-Dîn of Balkh," and he went out to meet him.

He was a great master. His main work, *'Awârif al-ma'ârif (The Book of Definitions)*, is still studied today. People came from all over the world to ask him for guidance and wrote to him exposing their problems. His doctrine was, at the time, deeply mystical and strictly orthodox, and exercised a great influence on men who were not sufis in the strict sense of the word. Two of them were Ibn Battûta, who was a judge and a traveler and yet received the *khirqa* (the rough monk's dress) of the *tarîqa* in Ispahan, and the Persian poet Sa'dî of Shiraz (1208–1292), who mentions the selfless love and the piety of Shihâb od-Dîn in his *Bûstân*. (See J. Trimingham, *Sufi Orders*, p. 36) Numerous branches are attached to that brotherhood, notably in India and Afghanistan.

The Shâdhilîya. This was to become the most important brotherhood in North Africa and in Egypt. It was founded by Abu'l Hassan 'Ali ash-Shâdhilî (1196–1258), who was a disciple of the celebrated 'Abd as-Salâm ibn Mashîsh, who was a disciple of Abû Madyan Shu'aib b.al Hussain (1126–1198) of Tlemcen, who was the greatest of the first masters of *tasawwuf*. Abû Madyan had met Ahmad ar-Rifâ'î in Iraq and lived in Bidjâya (Algiers). Among his spiritual sons we can cite the great Ibn ul-'Arabî (born in Andalusia and died in Damascus in 1240), Ibn Sab'în, and the poet Shustarî, whose poems are always recited in the *hadras* (meetings) of the shâdhilîs.

Abu'l-Hassan 'Ali ash-Shâdhilî was an ascetic man who led a life of contemplation and wandering. The master of a brotherhood in Morocco and persecuted in Tunisia because of his popularity, he fled to Egypt. There he was recognized at Al-Azhar and became the spiritual master of the 'ulamâ of Mecca. There are branches of this brotherhood in Istanbul, Rumania, The Comores, Egypt and North Africa. In Algiers there is an important branch in Miliana called the Youssefîya.

The Shâdhilîya counted among its disciples, Ibn 'Atâ Allah of Alexandria (d. 1309), the author of a volume of sufi aphorisms, *al-Hikam al-'Atâ'îya*, which is very famous and contains admirable prayers. Those of Ash-Shâdilî himself (*ahzâb*) are still used and recited during the *dhikrs* of his order.

The Kubrâwîya. This brotherhood is attached to Najm od-Dîn Kubrâ (1145–1221). Born in Khorassan, he received his first *khirqa* from the hands of Abû Najîb as-Sohrawardî in Egypt. He settled in his native province and had Bahâ-od-Dîn Walad, Rûmî's father, as a disciple and one of his six representatives. Another one of the six was Majd od-Dîn al Baghdâdî, who became the sheikh of the great Persian poet, Farîd ud-

Dîn'Attar (d. 1225), the author of, among other things, *Mantiq at-Tayr, The Divine Book* and *The Book of Secrets,* which he offered to the young Rûmî when the latter came to Nishâpur.

The order has flourished in Iran, the north of India, Kashmir and Baghdad.

The Naqshabandîya. This brotherhood came to be associated with the name of Muhammad Bahâ-od-Dîn an-Naqshabandî, but was actually started by Abû Ya'qûb Yûsuf al-Hamadânî (d. 1140) and was organized by 'Abd al-Khâliq al-Ghujdawanî (d. 1220). The Naqshabandîs practice a mental *dhikr* and prohibit public meetings and the *samâ'.* The exercises are ruled by 11 principles. The last three were established by Bahâ-od-Dîn an-Naqshabandî while the first eight were started by 'Abd al-Khâliq. The principle of this *tarîqa* is a concentration on the divine presence. This is accomplished by the silent repetition of the *shahâda* which is the Islamic profession of faith: *Lâ ilâha illâ'llâh.* "There is no God but God." During the recitation, one holds one's breath and follows a very precise technique.

The purpose of that was to revivify Islam by fighting against the deviations. It played a large role in the attachment of the Turks to the sunni tradition. The poet Djâmî belongs to this brotherhood. It had branches in Anatolia, the Caucasus and India.

The Rifâ'iiya. Founded by Ahmad ar-Rifâ'î (1106–1182), this brotherhood spread throughout Egypt and Syria. Until the 15th century, it was perhaps the most important brotherhood; later the Qâdirîya became more popular. Its reknown attracted a great number of sufis. Four of them created their own *tarîqas:* Badawîya, Dasûqîya, Shâdhilîya and 'Alwânîya.

The Rifâ'îya disciples engaged in ecstatic practices whose end was to prove the superiority of the spirit over the flesh. The great traveler, Ibn Battûta, gave us a report of the visit he made in 1327 to the *zâouia* in Wâsit when his caravan stopped there one day. "I therefore had the occasion to visit the tomb of the saint, Abu'l-Abbâs Ahmad ar-Rifâ'î, which is in a village called Umm'Ubaida, and which is one day's journey past Wâsit . . . It is a vast convent where thousands of poor disciples live . . . After the afternoon prayers, drums were beaten and the derviches started to dance. After they performed the sunset prayers, they brought the supper which consisted of bread, fish, milk and dates. When all had eaten and recited the first of the night prayers, they repeated the *dhikr* with the sheikh Ahmad sitting on a prayer rug belonging to his aforementioned ancestor. Then the concert started. They had prepared

Rifâ'îya disciples celebrating the new year. (Cairo, 1965)

bundles of firewood which they burned while they danced in the middle
of the flames. Some of them rolled in the fire, others put it in their
mouths, until they extinguished it totally. That is their habitual practice
and it is distinctive of the Ahmadî derviches. (*The Travels of Ibn
Battuta*, trad., H.A.R. Gibb, II, 273–274)

The Qâdirîya. This brotherhood was founded by 'Abd-al Qâdir al-
Jîlânî (1078–1166) who was born in Jîlân, near Baghdad. He was an
ascetic, a missionary and a professor, and lived teaching the highest
virtues of charity, without distinction of races or religions. Pious and
humble, he is the most revered saint in Islam. He had an immense
authority and the reputation of being a thaumaturge. Many of his
works have reached us, the most famous being *al-Ghunya li-tâlibî tarîq
al-Haqq,* which serves as a manual. The *tarîqa* has always been considered as irreproachably orthodox.

Baghdad remained for many centuries the center of attraction for this
powerful brotherhood. Independent groups were formed little by little.
Today we find branches in Iraq, Turkey, India, Turkestan, China,
Nubia, Sudan and North Africa.

The Sheikh Ahmad al-'Alawî (drawing by Frithjof Schuon)

The Khalwatîya. Asceticism and retreats are particularly stressed by this brotherhood, founded by 'Umar al-Khalwatî (d. 1397). It began in Syria and spread to Anatolia, Egypt and Hidjaz in Saudi Arabia; and scattered in many secondary brotherhoods. In the 17th century the *tarîqa* knew a new period of expansion. From Cairo, the disciples entered the eastern Sudan and soon the *takyas* covered North Africa.

These are the main *tarîqas* of old origin. The 19th century saw a renewal of the sufi orders, totally opposed to the Wahhâbî movement which preached a very strict and puritanical Islam, putting the accent on the absolute transcendence of God. Let us cite, among the brotherhoods of that period, the *tarîqa* Tadjânîya. Abu'l-'Abbâs al-Tidjânî, who was born in Algeria (1737–1815), refers himself to the Prophet directly. The brotherhood has spread primarily throughout Africa.

Founded at about the same time, the *tarîqa* Darqawîya (by Abu Hâmid al-'Arabî ad Darqâwî, 1760–1823) has become the most numerous of the Maghreb brotherhoods, and may be the most influential. It has many branches. The founder is buried in Fez. Another great sheikh, closer to us in time, is the sheikh Ahmad al-'Alawî of Mostaganem. He was a mystical poet (See M. Lings, *A Moslem Saint in the 20th Century*). Another of the brotherhoods derives from the Idrîsîya, which started with Ahmad Ibn Idrîs (1760–1837) of Fez, who became a great teacher in Mecca. The most important branch is perhaps the Sanûsîya in Libya and Syria.

The modern reformists have stressed certain negative aspects of the brotherhoods — maraboutism and over-passivity. Maraboutism, or the "cults of saints," represents a regrettable form of veneration. Sainthood naturally inspires, and also natural is the desire to ask for the intercession of men reknowned for their virtues, but orthodox Islam admits a recourse to God alone. Over-passivity, or quietism, is equated with a passive resignation regarding temporal destiny. Some brotherhoods, yielding to the pressure of the colonial powers, have signed pacts with them, which explains the distrust some Moslem governments have toward those brotherhoods.

These accusations are not altogether new; in Moslem history there have always been hostile currents toward sufism. Hanafite lawmakers and mou'tazilite theologians have never restrained from criticizing what they considered contrary to orthodoxy. It is essential, however, to assert that these attacks are justified only toward the *deviations* from sufism. Thus we find a thinker like Mohammad Iqbal pressing the sufis not to sit dreaming on the shore but to struggle with the waves, immortality being conquered only through this struggle. Iqbal also affirms that sufism is the highest form of Islamic spirituality. Today, the attachment to the fraternal fervor, which is the lifestyle of the *zâouias,* remains an active constituent of the religion, especially at the popular level. "The reality of it was never doubted, and it compensates for all the failures and calamities of history in the secret of the hearts." (L. Gardet, *Men of Islam*, p. 313)

The community of *Ikhwan* (brothers) united by the same spiritual thirst inside the *zâouia,* cannot naturally ignore the upheaval of the world outside. The brotherhood necessarily studies the assimilation of the group as a religious entity within a changing society, subjected to all the difficulties of a difficult modernity. We know that there is no monasticism in Islam, so their goal is not to lead a life of hermits. Their quest is much deeper; they want to live their élan toward God without renouncing their duties as citizens. It is a dangerous misunderstanding of their own culture which leads many Moslems today to question the role of the brotherhoods in the social structures and the process of development, whatever the economic options of the country may be. However, we do observe today a strong revival in most Islamic countries, of the mystical attraction toward the brotherhoods and the activities of their members.

Varying from region to region and from brotherhood to brotherhood, there are two categories of *tarîqas* today. In some, the proposed goal is for the members to attain an authentic mystical experience by means of a rigorous discipline inspired by the Koranic Word and the sheikh's guidance. This discipline is based primarily on prayers and recitations of God's Names as well as on asceticism and dedication to the community. This category remains specifically religious, fairly closed and preoccupied with the sole purpose of attaining an experience of God.

Other brotherhoods propose to perpetuate a religious climate around the memory of a saint, founder or follower of a *tarîqa*. Such *tarîqas* were active in the past, teaching theology and the Koran. Colonization and a certain stagnation in the practice have often "dimmed" the spirit of the *tarîqas,* which therefore lost their essential functions. In current times, the religious person in charge welcomes the believers and organizes periodic festivals to recall a saint's piety. He is chosen because of his links to the deceased Master, and especially because of his virtue and his wisdom. He generously gives advice to the men and women who come to talk to him about their worries and their hopes. The ambiance of peace and silence which generally reign there is very strong during the prayers and the *dhikrs* that they perform. The hearts of the believers in the villages and towns, without distinction and without necessarily belonging to the *tarîqa,* are in unison with the rhythms of the sacred verses of the Koran.

We can measure thus, all that the Moslem personality can gain by partaking in an interiority which reminds the workers and the students of their profound identity as believers; members of an immense community. This fortification is valuable to these people in their daily lives. Confronted by a world haunted by the ghost of absurdity, the highest message of the Islamic faith is not to remain fixed in a vain nostalgia for the past, or to be seduced by a faceless technology. The great masters of sufism have always urged not to run away from the realities, but to confer to these their real dimension — to fill them with their spiritual meaning. If the sufis like to repeat that "the heart of the believer is the highest heaven," they do not forget the Word of the Prophet: "The whole earth is a mosque."

Tidjanîya zâouia near Toggourt (Algiers).

Notes

1. See *Encyclopedia of Islam*, article *Tarîqa*.
2. R.-A. Nicholson: *Studies in Islamic Mysticism*.
3. *Kûn*: Be, this is the "Fiat that creates," according to the Koran. (In Arabic it is written with the letters Kâf and Nûn.)
4. "At the distance of twice the range of an arrow." (Koran, LIII, 9): this refers to the Angel Gabriel who appeared to the Prophet Mohammad during a particular revelation in that manner.
5. We have come across the two meanings of that word, which designates the brotherhood, and the Spiritual Path. It is in the latter that the word is used here.
6. H. Nasr, *Islam, Perspectives and Realities*, chapter 5.
7. H. Nasr, *op. cit.*, p. 194.
8. H. Nasr, *op. cit.*, p. 171.
9. See J. Spencer Trimingham, *The Sufi Orders*, p. 160.
10. 'Ali, The son-in-law of the Prophet, and the fourth Caliph, and as such called here, the Commander of the Believers.
11. Text established by W. Chittick, *The Sufi Doctrine of Rûmî*, p. 64-65.
12. *Mystique et Poesie en Islam*, p. 63 by Eva de Vitray-Meyerovitch.
13. It is unfortunately impossible to do more than evoke the memory of the innumerable saints, who, in Islam, took the Path of *Tasawwuf*, from Hassan el-Bakri (d. 728), Rabi'a al-Adawyya, also from Basra and his contemporary, who sung the divine love in marvelous poems, to all the sufis known or unknown, we encounter during the centuries. Farid-od-Dîn 'Attar, among others, gives a vibrant testimony about some of them, in his *Memorial of Saints*.

"O Hadrat Mawlânâ!" – *"O The Sacred Presence of Mawlânâ!"*

Index

Chronology

Bibliography

Works of Djalâl-od-Dîn Rûmî

Dîvan-e Shams-e Tabrîz, édition Forûzânfar, Téhéran, 1958–1962. Traduction française partielle, sous le titre Odes mystiques, par E. de Vitray-Meyerovitch, avec la collaboration de M. Mokri, Klincksieck, Paris, 1973.

Fîhi-mâ-fîhî (le Livre du Dedans), traduction française par E. de Vitray-Meyerovitch, éditions Sindbad, Paris, 1976.

Mathnawî, édition et traduction anglaise par R. A. Nicholson, 8 volumes, Leyde, 1925. — Traduction française en préparation aux éditions Sindbad par E. de Vitray-Meyerovitch.

On Rûmî

Aflâkî, Shams-ol-Dîn, Manâqib ul-'ârifîn (les Saints des derviches-tourneurs), traduction C. Huart, 2 volumes, Paris, 1918.

Chittick, W.-C., The Sufi doctrine of Rûmî, Téhéran, 1974.

Friedlander, I., The whirling dervishes, Collier Books, New York, 1975.

Nicholson, R.-A., Rûmî, poet and mystic, Londres, Allen and Unwin, 1950.

Ritter, H., "Das Proomium des Matnawî-i Maulawî," ZDM, 93-1932, p. 169-196. — "Der Reigen der Tanzenden Derwische," Zeitschrift für Vergleichende Musikwissenschaft, 1-1933, p. 28-40. — "Maulana Galaladdin Rûmî und sein Kreis," Der Islam, 26-1942, p. 116-158, 221-249. — "Der Mevlânafeier in Konya," Oriens, xv-1962, p. 248 s.

Schimmel, A. M., Die Bildersprache Dshellâaddîn Rûmî, Walldorf-Hassan, Verlag für Orientkunde, 1949.

Teymourtache, I., le Mysticisme de Djalâl-od-Dîn Rûmî, thèse universitaire, dactylographiée, Paris, 1952.

Vitray-Meyerovitch, E. de, Mystique et Poésie en Islam: Djalâl-od-Dîn Rûmî et l'ordre des derviches tourneurs, Desclée de Brouwer, Paris, 2nd éd., 1973.

Numerous studies in Persian and Turkish and an exhaustive bibliography by Mehmet Onder in Turkish.

On Sufism in General

Le Qor'ân, traduction D. Masson, Hamidullah, Pickthall.

'Affifi, A.-E., The Mystical Philosophy of Muhyid-Dîn Ibn-ul-'Arabî, Cambridge, 1939.

Al Hujwîrî, Ali b 'Uthman, Kashf-ul-Mahjüb, traduction Nicholson, Londres, Luzac, 1911.

Ansârî al-Harawî, 'Abd Allâh, Kitâb-Manâzil as-sa'irîn (les Étapes des itinérants vers Dieu), traduction S. Laugier de Beaurecueil, Paris-Le Caire, 1962.

Arberry, A. J., le Soufisme, traduction J. Gouillard, Paris, "Cahiers du Sud," 1952.

Ardalan, N. et Bakhtiyar, L., The Sense of Unity: The Sufi Tradition in Persian Architecture, Chicago, 1971.

Arnold, Sir Thomas, The Preaching of Islam, Londres, Luzac, 1935.

'Attar, Farîd-od-Dîin, Mantiq-Uttâr (le Langage des Oiseaux), traduction Garcin de Tassy, Paris, 1857. — Ilahy Nâma (le Livre divin), traduction F. Rouhani, Paris, Albin Michel, 1961. — Tadhkirat-ul-Awliya (le Mémorial des Saints), traduction A. Pavet de Courteille, Paris, Le Seuil, 1976.

Burckhardt, T., *Introduction aux doctrines ésotériques de l'Islam,* Alger, Messerschmitt, 1955. — Traduction des *Fuçûç al-Hikam (la Sagesse des prophètes) d'Ibn-ul 'Arabî,* Paris, Albin Michel, 1955.
Dermenghem, Émile, *l'Éloge du vin,* traduction de *Al Khamriya de 'Omar Ibn Al-Faridh,* Paris, Vega, 1931. — *Mahomet et la tradition islamique,* Paris, Le Seuil, 1955.
Djamî, *Lawâ'ih, a treatise on sûfism,* traduction Whinfield et Kazvînî, Londres, 1906.
Farmer, H.-G., *History of Arab music to the 13th century,* Londres, Luzac, 1929.
Gardet, L., *l'Islam,* Paris, Desclée de Brouwer, 1970. — *Les Hommes de l'Islam,* Paris, Hachette, 1977.
Iqbal, M., *Reconstruire la pensée religieuse de l'Islam,* traduction E. de Vitray-Meyerovitch, Paris, A. Maisonneuve, 1955. — *Payâm-e Mashriq (Message de l'Orient),* traduction E. de Vitray-Meyerovitch et M. Achena, Paris, les Belles Lettres, 1956. — *Djâvîd-Nâma (le Livre de l'Éternité,* traduction E. de Vitray-Meyerovitch, et M. Mokri, Albin Michel, 1962. — *The Development of metaphysics in Persia,* traduction E. de Vitray-Meyerovitch, sous presse, Paris, Sindbad.
Lings, M., *Qu'est-ce que le soufisme?* traduction R. Du Pasquier, Paris, Le Seuil, 1977.
Massignon, L., Oeuvres complètes et notamment: *Essai sur les origines du lexique technique de la mystique musulmane,* Paris, Vrin, 1968. — *La Passion d'al-Hallâj,* Gallimard, 1976.
Monawwar, Mohammad Ebn E., *Asrar at-Tawhîd fi maqâmât ash Sheikh Abû Sa'îd (Les Étapes mystiques de Shaykh Abû Sa'îd),* traduction M. Achena, Paris, Desclée de Brouwer, 1974.
Nasr, S. H., *Three Muslim Sages,* Cambridge Mass., 1964. — *Sufi essays,* Londres, Allen and Unwin, 1972. — *Islam, perspectives et réalités,* Paris, Buchet-Chastel, 1975.
Nicholson, R.-A., *Studies in Islamic Mysticism,* Cambridge, 1921. — *The Idea of personality in Sufism,* Cambridge, 1923. — *The Mystics of Islam,* Londres, Routledge and Kegan Paul, 1963.
Sanâ'î, *Hadîqat al-haqîqa (les Jardins des vérités).*
Shabestarî, M., *Gulshan-î-râz (la Roseraie de Mystères),* traduction anglaise E.-H. Whinfield, Londres, 1880.
Smith, M., *Râbi'a the Mystic and her fellow-saints in Islam,* Cambridge, 1928.
Walad, Bahâ-ud-Dîn, *Ma'ârif,* 3 volumes, édition de l'Université, Istanbul.
Walad, Sultân, *Walad-Nâma,* édition de Homâi, Téhéran.
Encyclopédie de l'Islam, article "Tarîqa," Leiden-Paris, 1954.

On the brotherhoods in the world today

Trimingham, J.-S., *The Sufi orders in Islam,* Oxford, Clarendon Press, 1971.
Mustapha Cherif, *Dynamique de la zâouia de Sidi Ahmed Benyoucef dans l'Algérie moderne,* thèse de doctorat, Paris, 1977.